LEITNER STRIKES

LEITNER STRIKES

by **Ted Leitner**
with **Chris Cobbs**

AVANT BOOKS™   Oak Tree

Copyright 1985 Ted Leitner

All rights reserved under International and Pan-American
Copyright Conventions, including the right to reproduce this book
or portions thereof in any form whatsoever except for use by a
reviewer in connection with a review.

ISBN 0-932238-31-9
Library of Congess Catalog Card Number 85-71447

Co-published by:

Avant Books™   Oak Tree Publications
Slawson Communications, Inc.   9601 Aero Drive, Suite 202
3719 Sixth Avenue   San Diego, CA 92123
San Diego, CA 92103-4316

Cover design by Ed Roxburgh, The Word Shop, San Diego
Interior design by Mike Kelly, The Word Shop, San Diego
Editorial coordination by Linnea Dayton, Avant Books
Cover photo by Rodney C. Jones, Inc., San Diego

Printed in U.S.A.

CONTENTS

CHAPTER 1

The Firing Line

I thought I was going to die. The fifth game of the 1984 World Series had just ended, and with it, the San Diego Padres' chances of writing one of the more improbable chapters of baseball history. Of course, the season had been little short of miraculous anyway. From a San Diego perspective, what the Padres had done in winning the National League West by 12 games and then defeating the Chicago Cubs in a dramatic best-of-five series, was undoubtedly the pinnacle of the city's professional sports history.

I had just concluded my visit to the Padre locker room for the postgame interviews (one of my *least* favorite chores as a broadcaster). Along the way I've conducted hundreds, probably thousands of interviews with exhausted, sweaty, often ill-tempered jocks. When a team loses a climactic game, as the Padres had just done, the discomfort is amplified for the men on both sides of the camera. I think I would rather have oral surgery than do the typical postgame show.

But there I was outside of Tiger Stadium, making my way to a site across the street where we were going to do our live report via satellite for the 5 o'clock news on KFMB-TV. It was a cold, dismal afternoon in mid-October, and downtown Detroit was going berserk.

Along with my cameraman, I had to fight my way through a mob that was on the verge of erupting into a riot. Now, maybe we're not talking riot on the scale of what happened in Motown in 1967 when one of the century's worst urban riots broke out. But this was beginning to seem like a dangerous facsimile.

Ironically, we were going to be doing the show from a church rooftop. We approached the ladder we would have to climb to get an aerial shot of the celebration. Somehow, we were managing to make our way with a camera through thousands of Detroit lunatics. (Excuse me, I realize that's redundant.) Anyway, as you probably know, the little light on a TV camera produces a moth-to-the-flame effect. You turn on the light and all the local insects flock right to it.

I was afraid they would find out we were San Diegans and decide to kill us a as part of the festivities All around us there were policemen with riot helmets, plexiglas facemasks, and long clubs that they were poking into people's stomachs. And I kept thinking to myself, "This is a riot, Ted, a goddam riot." At the church, we wasted no time scrambling up the ladder toward the relative safety of the roof. Just as we stepped out on the roof, some idiots stopped a police car and dragged the cops out of it. Unreal. Then they overturned the car and set it on fire. As I began my live report, I heard the tires exploding.

At about the same moment a motorcyclist came by, and the mob surrounded him and tossed the cycle on the fire. Then they really got crazy. The rioters ransacked four taxis and a Greyhound bus. We found out later the bus was full of senior citizens from Cleveland. Whenever I make a speech at a civic club or some function, I tell the audience that I have this image of a fence

2

trying to sell hundreds of pairs of orthopedic shoes, dentures, and hearing aids. That would have been the booty stolen from the luggage from the Greyhound bus, which was left behind, a burned-out hulk.

From our vantage point we watched as mounted policemen advanced in a line toward the rioters, who were pelting the horses with bottles and debris. One horse got belted on the head with a green glass Rolling Rock bottle. And there I was, describing it all live to the folks in San Diego. I said something like, "Would you look at those morons!" Back in San Diego, I was informed by station management that a Michigan state senator had been visiting in Southern California and had seen the broadcast. This senator wanted to sue because I had alledgedly defamed the city of Detroit. Imagine that! He would have had a heckuva tough time in court trying to prove they *weren't* morons. I'd still like to meet that gentleman and remind him of what the comedian Fred Allen said of Detroit: "Two Newarks, without the glitter."

If you don't mind going off on a little tangent with me here, I'd like to demonstrate how stupid I once was. The only time I was fired from a job in my life was when I worked in Philadelphia in the late 1970s. In the aftermath, I nearly wound up taking a position in Detroit. During the 1984 World Series, I thought about that often. I could have been living (if you could call it that) in that place for the past eight years. While I watched the idiots burning the police cars, I thought, "You lucky bastard. Look at what you've spared yourself."

The way it developed, I flew to Detroit for a job interview the week after Thanksgiving in 1977. That's standard protocol in broadcasting. Management fires, you just after you've returned from vacation, having

having spent your life's savings. Or they fire you at Thanksgiving or Christmas, times when everyone just loves to be out on the pavement hustling for a job. It's terribly clever the way they break the bad news. Typically, the station honcho will stop by your desk and say, "Got a minute?" That's broadcasting code for "Would you like a blindfold and a cigarette?" "Got a minute?" is inevitably followed by the coy phrase, "We gotta make a change." You know they don't mean the weatherman.

The problem in Philadelphia began when the boys upstairs finished some audience marketing research. The results were fascinating. The research proved people are not all the same. In my previous job, in Hartford, Connecticut, they had done some similar research, the recurring theme of which was, "Gee, Leitner is so enthusiastic, I really like him, he's always smiling." In Philadelphia the research disclosed an unfortunate variation. "Why is he always smiling?" people asked. "Doesn't he know the Flyers lost?" Sports is not a laughing matter in the City of Brotherly Love, as I discovered the hard way. Philadelphia is only a couple hundred miles from Hartford, but human nature sure undergoes some dramatic changes in that distance. When they fired me in Philadelphia, they gave me until January 1 to find another job.

I had never been let go before. In Philadelphia I'd sensed I was in trouble. But there's a mechanism in the mind of a broadcaster that won't allow him to think he's no good. It's analogous to a ballplayer trying to hit a baseball. There's no way a hitter is going to touch Nolan Ryan's fast ball if he doubts his own ability to swing the bat. Similarly, there's just no way a broadcaster can communicate at all if he's scared or short on confidence when he gets out there in front of the camera and lights. So you hide your doubts from yourself.

Just a month earlier I had been on the cover of the Sunday TV supplement of a Delaware newspaper. That had thrown me off. The paper had gone through the TV station's promotions department to set up the interview. I figured the promotions people would know if I was walking death and would have so advised the reporter assigned to write about me. There was no way I could envision my colleagues being so devious as to allow the story to appear, knowing full well I was about to be axed. So I assumed I was safe for the time being. And then a few weeks later, I heard those three magic words. "Got a minute?"

Fortunately, I had some friends in the TV business, and through one of them I was able to get a job interview at the CBS affiliate in Detroit. As I said, it was late November, and my plane landed in a blinding snowstorm. The only thing I'd ever seen that could compare was a storm in Hartford, when the plane kept taxiing through a blizzard for what seemed like a half hour. Finally the pilot came on the intercom and said, "Look, if anybody knows where the terminal is, don't hesitate to inform the stewardess, because I can't find it." Nobody laughed. It was the kind of flight where passengers break into a spontaneous cheer after the wheels touch down safely. You're just grateful to be alive. This Detroit landing ran a close second to that one in Hartford.

It took me about an hour to make the drive in my rented Pinto from the snowbanked airport to the TV station in suburban Southfield. I pulled up, and through driving snow I could vaguely discern the outlines of a building that looked sort of like Buchenwald. I mean this literally. There was barbed wire and a guard tower, and they required employees to insert a little card in the electrified doors to gain admittance. After the '67 riots and the auto industry calamities, I guess they figured nobody was safe, even in the suburbs.

My job interview was rather anticlimactic after all this build-up. The next day I boarded another airplane, this one headed for San Diego. Another pal had lined up an interview at KFMB. We landed in sunny 65-degree weather under blue skies, and I thought, "*This* is more like it."

After my interview came a brief episode of California culture shock. The news director took me to a local sandwich shop for lunch, and my Club Deluxe came with sprouts. "What the hell is this?" I said. "There's a patch of somebody's lawn on my sandwich." I thought of the comic who does the routine about the pizza with orange slices and avocado and sprouts. I 'd never seen a sandwich like this where I grew up, which was in Yonkers, New York. I was, and am, quite an authority on anything gastronomic, provided it comes between two pieces of bread. I didn't believe there was any serious sandwich lover who would consider eating sprouts. More about this later.

When it came time to decide where I was going to relocate, Detroit or San Diego, there were several things to consider. While working in Philadelphia, I'd been commuting to Los Angeles on weekends to visit my son, who was living with my ex-wife in Orange County. I'd spend Saturday night and Sunday with my son, then hop the red-eye back to Philadelphia. With a stopover in Cleveland, the plane usually arrived at 7 a.m. on Monday. I would work five days and then make the transcontinental leap again the following weekend. The San

Diego climate was a real lure, and so was the proximity to Orange County. I would be only 90 minutes from my son. The offer in Detroit was for $50,000, compared to $30,000 in San Diego, but a lot of the difference was going to be eaten up by airplane fares in a year's time. The salary difference was meaningless, so I took the job at KFMB. Eight years later, at the World Series, it crossed my mind that I could have been freezing my butt off and dodging broken bottles in Detroit for the better part of a decade. Of course, I might have been fired, or dead, within a year in Detroit. I don't really know if they would have bought my act in Detroit anymore than they had in Philadelphia.

I'm a pretty irreverent guy most of the time, and I don't know if it would have worked in the Motor City. Judging from what I saw on TV during the World Series, I doubt it. The most irreverent sports commentator I saw was a guy named Al Ackerman, and he was relatively tame. The only thing he had ever done that raised an eyebrow was a mock interview with a former coach of the Detroit Lions, Tommy Hudspeth. Hudspeth would not talk to broadcast guys after a Lions game because he had a radio show with exclusive rights to him, so only the newspaper men got the benefit of his insight, such as it was. Ackerman got the rather inspired idea to simulate a live interview with Hudspeth in the studio. What he did was to rig up a dummy with a Lions cap and a whistle around his neck. When the camera zoomed in, Ackerman said, "It's very hard to get an interview with this man unless you pay him, but we'll see what we can get out of him. So, tell us, coach, what was your game plan? What did you think of the opposition?" All the cliché questions, all followed by silence. A pretty hilarious routine, I have to admit.

In spite of this one lively moment, Ackerman struck me as being generally a honker for the Tigers in the World Series. He was the guy who had come up with the catch phrase, "Bless you, boys." He had originated it on a sarcastic note several years ago when the Tigers were struggling. He would say, "Well, folks, the Tigers lost again today, 5-1. Bless you, boys." It didn't really catch on until 1984, when the Tigers became the darlings of Detroit, and Manager Sparky Anderson appropriated the refrain for the title of a book he wrote to celebrate the season. Thinking this over, I realized I would not have lasted in a blue-collar town like Detroit, where they view pro sports as the be-all and end-all. Detroit is really just Philadelphia Northwest. My style would not have made it there. So, I was lucky that my greed had not dragged me to Detroit in 1977.

I know I have a reputation for being critical, but I'm quite different from many transplanted easterners, who tend to knock whatever city they're in west of the Mississippi. I adapted to San Diego right off, and I never looked back to the distant east. I never compared San Diego with Philadelphia or New York. Very early in my broadcasting career, when I was a college boy out of Yonkers working summers in the Midwest, I had learned a valuable lesson. I was working for a radio station in the tiny Oklahoma town of Cushing. I'd bitch and moan to the station manager about having to crouch with a bulky tape recorder in a dimly lit stadium on a Friday night and describe the action of the local high school team for broadcast the next day. My boss gave me some good advice. "Hey, we don't want to listen to you complaining," he said. "This is Cushing, and we don't really care how it was back in New York City. Remember, wherever you are, don't start off telling people what it was like where you came from. Nobody wants to hear that stuff." I'll admit it — when I was working alongside anchorman Mike Tuck at Channel 8, I occasionally told a few short Philadelphia stories. But they were never to build up Philadelphia or belittle San Diego.

I know, a lot of people from back east say there's no theater, no culture, nothing to do at night in San Diego. I've heard all that, and some of it may be true. But I loved the sunshine and the lifestyle from the instant I first stepped off that plane in November, 1977. A bright, breezy, 65-degree day in mid-December eases any residue of culture shock and makes it all seem worthwhile. Besides, it didn't take me long to get into the habit of saying, "Ham and cheese. No sprouts."

CHAPTER 2

The Perils of the Ivory Tower

As we all know, the Padres didn't do so well in the World Series. But my opinion is that it didn't really matter. They were playing a better team, and there was never any doubt in my mind that they were going to lose. But after the National League playoffs, it didn't make that much difference what happened in the Series. It was essentially an anticlimax. Oh, sure, there would have been have a big parade and San Diego would have gone semi-batty. But there was no way the Padres were losers after what they had accomplished in the playoffs.

Having said this, I think it's kosher to repeat the prize line that emerged from the World Series. Know why the San Diego pitchers failed so miserably against Detroit? Basically, it was because the San Diego pitching staff gagged under the pressure, and pitching coach Norm Sherry didn't know the Heimlich maneuver. You might have noticed that Sherry got reassigned to the minors even though it wasn't entirely fair to blame him for what happened to the likes of Eric Show, Ed Whitson, Goose Gossage, and the rest.

Since we've already established that winning and losing are not the only things that count, let me say right here that the postgame scene is one thing that does matter to most of us media types. It matters less to me than to many broadcasters, because I don't have to go to the athletes for interviews except after really big games when I'm involved in the radio broadcast. That was the case in the 1984 playoffs. By the time the Padres reached the postseason tournament, other broadcasters were taking bets on who, if anyone, would talk to me.

My problem is, a lot of ballplayers don't like me. Neither do a lot of managers, coaches, general managers, owners, agents, players' wives, and everyday, run-of-the-mill fans.

You know what? Who cares? My responsibility is to my audience. My responsibility is to tell the truth. And that makes one helluva lot of people in sports unhappy.

So the betting line among my broadcasting buddies had it that no more than about three Padres were likely to talk to me in an official-type interview for the playoffs or the World Series. If Garry Templeton, for example, happened to hit a game-winning homerun, I was going to be in big trouble. I doubt that Tempy would say a word if he saw me lying by the side of the road, dying. He may be extreme in this respect, but in the final analysis, most of his teammates approved of his stance. As I said, there were very few Padres left who would oblige when I held out the mike in front of them.

I'm pretty much past the stage where I have to count on players to give me quotes. I've paid my dues, so I don't have to visit the clubhouse except in rare cases, such as the postseason. Basically, I'm allowed to stay in my ivory tower and deliver my commentaries without fearing the consequences of athletes refusing to speak to me. That's a privilege few journalists enjoy, but

I've earned it. I have the insulation I need to deliver my daily spiel. Other commentators have the same protection. Take Bill Moyers of CBS. He can't sit next to Dan Rather and do a scathing commentary on Ed Meese and then be expected to visit the White House the next day and get an interview with Meese. It doesn't work that way.

One of my colleagues in the TV sports biz, Mike Smith, once made a rather dumb comment about me: "Leitner is always knocking the Chargers, but you never see him at practice," Smith said. Let me tell you something. I've seen more football teams practice and done more play-by-play than Mike Smith ever dreamed of. To criticize me for something I do wrong — and there's plenty — is fine. But don't say I criticize the Chargers because I don't go to their practices. That implies that I'm afraid, and that's just baloney. What am I expected to do? If I see the Chargers kicking ass in practice, am I therefore to conclude that they have a good team and they've just been hiding it at game time these last two years? Am I supposed to decide that trading a draft choice for two salamis named Abdul Salaam and Kenny Neil wasn't really such a bad deal? I guess if I saw more practices, I would realize they really do have a pretty good defense, huh? That kind of misguided knock just blows me away.

It's obvious why a guy like Mike Smith never criticizes the Chargers. It's because he does some preseason TV games and hosts the Don Coryell highlight show. He needs to be Don's friend. He doesn't want to make Don mad. And when a broadcaster is more concerned about being patted on the back by the people he's supposed to be covering, the audience is being cheated. Going to 8000 practices has nothing to do with telling the truth about a team.

Anyway, going into the World Series, I knew I was going to be responsible for getting some stuff in the locker room after each game. And I was hoping that Steve Garvey, Tim Flannery, or Kurt Bevacqua would do something. I knew I was in trouble if Templeton or Alan Wiggins, or any of the John Birchers played a key role in a game.

I'd got into trouble with three pitchers, Dave Dravecky, Mark Thurmond and Eric Show, when I did a less than glowing commentary on the John Birch Society during the regular season. The players had done an interview with the *Los Angeles Times* in which they discussed their involvement in the group, and it became a very controversial issue.

I knew there was going to be trouble when Jan Dravecky called me at the station even before I went on the air to deliver my commentary. She told me how "fair" she thought I usually was, as if that would stop me from being critical, or something.

I delivered what I thought was a fairly light segment, beginning by saying that these guys had a right to belong to any legal group they chose. But when it came to the reaction of their black teammates, I thought there could be problems in terms of disrupting team unity. I then added that I did not like the John Birch Society, which I viewed as a myopic, fanatic organization. This country is based on political and religious tolerance. Even though you find somebody's views abhorrent, a person has a right to spout his or her views in public. But, I stressed, the Birch Society membership talks of wiping out communists, and preaches vigilance, and is generally intolerant of anyone who doesn't buy their party line.

The team was out of town when the story broke,

and so they missed my commentary. But they heard about it, third-hand, in the usual distorted, twisted manner. Show, Dravecky and Thurmond thought I was being inflammatory. Thurmond went so far as to tell another broadcaster he wasn't going to talk to me until I apologized to him. I had nothing to apologize for. The Birchers say they're such loyal Americans, but then they see someone with a different view and they demand an apology. According to my understanding of the Constitution, we're all allowed to have an opinion and to deliver it in lawful assembly without having to apologize. I find it antithetical for the Birchers to say, "I love America, and you better love it, too, the exact way I do. You better dress and talk and cut your hair short just as I do. If you don't, you're disloyal." Sorry. I can't go for that. If Mark Thurmond is still waiting for an apology, I suggest he stop now and breathe deeply.

My differences with Templeton were not so philosophical, but they were just as deeply felt. The following incident occurred after a game several years ago. The Padres had played the Philadelphia Phillies, and a concert by the Beach Boys followed the game. I was involved in the radio broadcast that day, and since I didn't care to stick around for the concert, I was leaving the stadium well before most of the crowd. Templeton had the same idea, I guess. As I headed for the exit, I saw him about 20 yards ahead of me.

Tempy was approaching the parking lot when two little kids approached him with ballpoint pens and Padre caps. It was easy for me to remember what it was like to be 10 years old and walk up to a player for an autograph. It would make your whole day, and then some, to get the autograph.

As the first kid walked toward Garry, he didn't

even break stride. "No autographs," he grunted. Second kid, same thing. There was no way Templeton could hide behind the old excuse that if he stopped to sign for one kid, he'd be detained by dozens more. There was nobody around but those two little kids. Everyone else was inside waiting for the Beach Boys. Yet Templeton wouldn't sign two bubblegum cards.

Maybe he had rules for this kind of situation. On a trip to St. Louis I'd heard him tell another autograph seeker he had a rule against signing in the state of Missouri. I guess he was still bothered by his unpleasant experiences when he was with the Cardinals. It had sounded clever at the time, but I'm sure it wouldn't have amused an eight-year-old Little Leaguer, who could hardly share the responsibility for Templeton's struggles with St. Louis Manager Whitey Herzog.

I don't mean to single out Garry Templeton here. I've seen the same sort of boorish behavior from entirely too many ballplayers. In 1984 spring training, the California Angels visited Yuma for an exhibition game. Doug DeCinces stood there telling youngsters he wouldn't sign bubblegum cards. Fred Lynn refused to sign cards showing him in a Boston uniform. Bobby Grich wouldn't sign Oriole cards. This behavior struck me as typical of the Angels, who were the biggest gang of spoiled, over-the-hill ballpark millionaires in baseball history. A team with less heart and less unity than any I have ever seen. A purchased team of fatcats and egomaniacs. They could always talk a good game about how professional they were, but in truth they were a pack of dogs.

It makes me angry to witness this sort of ungrateful, prima donna autograph crap. Naturally I had to say something on the air the day after the Templeton episode. In retrospect, I was overly fair about it, because I didn't even use his name. I simply referred to him as a prominent Padre player who stiffed these two kids out of autographs. Garry obviously heard about it, because he relayed a graphic message through Terry Kennedy about what I could do to myself, and it was anatomically impossible. Templeton has never talked to me since.

Neither has Alan Wiggins, who was tight with Templeton. Once at Dodger Stadium I asked Wiggins to do a postgame show, and he just rolled his eyes and looked at the ground. At least he didn't tell me to do something unnatural, as Templeton had. I never got to know Wiggins very well, so I can't give you any real insight into the problems that led to his suspension for cocaine. That's a general problem I'll go into at length later on.

Even for a broadcaster who's on good terms with the jocks, it's damn near impossible to get a postgame guest if you don't offer a gift. It's an unofficial rule: you must have a present. I'm not sure if there's a minimum value, but try getting an interview if you can't produce a watch or a gift certificate. I remember one time we had Bill Virdon, who was then managing the Houston Astros, as our postgame guest. The prize was a $300 watch. He seemed shocked. I don't know where he'd been hiding, but Virdon's reaction was, "This is for me?" He couldn't get over it. Most players, however, would have grabbed the box without so much as a thank you. I'm going to be generous and concede that maybe there's some logic in the guest getting a little something, since the announcer and the station are getting paid. Maybe the athletes deserve something, too. On the other hand, maybe they should take the exposure, which often multiplies endorsement offers and banquet speech multiplies endorsement offer and banquet speech opportunities, and shut their mouths.

A fairly major part of the story of what happened to the Padres in the World Series had to do with pitching, and there was no way for me to get anything from guys like Thurmond or Show. I was pretty much reduced to sticking a shotgun mike in their face from the periphery of the circle of broadcasters standing by the player's cubicle. Anyway, I don't make my living as an interviewer except on these rare occasions. And I won't change to accommodate the athletes. I won't lie and say a guy goes to left real well and makes his own clothes and is popular with everybody. I am never going to be the standard, ass-kissing broadcaster just so I can get a swell interview. I'm convinced the audience would rather hear some opinions from me instead of 20 seconds with Don Coryell saying, "He's an awfully tough guy, really excellent." Nobody wants to hear that crap.

CHAPTER 3

Save Your Pythons, Please

I know it seems like I'm always bitching about something. I have clashed with just about everybody who's anybody in San Diego athletics over the past eight years. And I've clashed with San Diego populace at large who just felt the urge to pick up the phone, or pen and paper, and get something off their chest. Being one of the most visible targets in the city is fine up to a point. When people stop watching and listening, my career is in trouble. It's necessary for me to have a thick hide, and I do. Now I want to describe what it's like to be on my end — the receiving end.

Several years ago I got a letter that caught my eye right off because it had no return address. In a rough, scratchy hand it was addressed simply to "Asshole, in care of Channel 8, San Diego." And, wouldn't you know, the kid in our mail room delivered it to me. I asked him if he'd read it first. Nope, he'd just figured it was meant for me on the basis of all the other weird stuff that's intended for Leitner. He just *assumed* this garbage belonged on my desk.

I'm no different from anyone else. I want to be liked and admired. When I hear some celebrity, or semi-celebrity, say he doesn't care what's written about him as long as the name is spelled right, my reaction is "baloney." I care! I remember the first nasty column ever written about me. I was working in Hartford, Connecticut, in the early 1970s. The column was headlined, "Leitner Striking Out." It began by quoting what H. L. Mencken once said, how nobody ever went broke by underestimating the intelligence of the American public, and Channel 3, which I was on, certainly wasn't doing so. The critic proceeded to say I was a fine on-screen performer, but I left out too many scores. That was definitely a precursor of what I would be hearing repeatedly in years to come.

I couldn't finish reading that column. I guess I discovered how some athletes must feel when they're ripped apart by the press, or by me. My knees ached, and so did my heart. It was liked reading a Dear John letter. This is the feeling all of us in the public eye experience when we're criticized, and a six- or seven-figure income doesn't eliminate the pain.

Every now and then I get some wacko comment in person. My least favorite was at a 7-11 in Mission Beach. It happened a few years ago when NBC was showing a mini-series based on Norman Mailer's book about Gary Gilmore. The night before on the series, a firing squad had executed Gilmore. I was paying for some milk and bread when this guy walked up to me and said, "You watch that Gilmore thing? That should've been you."

I can be quick at times, but at that moment, it was like I'd been slapped in the face. I didn't have anything to say. I just stood there. Other people in the store heard it and groaned, it was in such bad taste. All I could think to do was simply walk away.

Another time I was at a San Diego State basketball game and I was talking to Linden King, the Charger linebacker. As we waited for the game to start, we were approached by a stranger. He took up a position and held his ground while I thought, "What does this idiot want? Maybe he'll look at Linden and figure he's my bodyguard." No such luck. After a few minutes I interrupted my conversation with Linden and turned to the stranger.

"May I help you?" I tried to be short with him.

"I hate your guts!" the guy said in earnest.

This was another occasion when the snappy rejoinder eluded me. I muttered something like "OK" and resumed my chat with Linden. My son, who was at the game with me, looked up at me with eyes as big as half-dollars when the interloper snarled out his feelings.

"You don't do enough hockey," he continued.

That cleared up the mystery. I knew there had to be some reason this fellow hated me. I took my son's hand, and we went off to find our seats. As we were walking away, our friend muttered something I didn't catch. Later, my son told me the guy had called me "a fat bastard."

It gets worse.

One time a guy loosened the lug nuts on the wheels of my car. A local dealership had loaned me a new car in 1981. It was brand-new, fresh from the factory. And damned if somebody didn't mess with the tires. My ex-wife happened to be driving the car down National City Boulevard — I wasn't there — when one of the wheels popped right off. She had it repaired and then drove back to the dealer, who reasoned that someone had been fooling around with the lug nuts. Some joker was apparently trying to kill me.

That was my scariest moment, but there have been others. Lots of telephone threats. I seem to get them like other people get calls from friends. "You're dead." That's all. A voice will come on and tell me that. Or, "You're history." These conversations don't last much longer than it takes me to replace the receiver.

I get threats by mail, too. They don't come with little letters cut out of a magazine and pasted on a sheet of paper. You'd only see that stuff in a television thriller. I do, however, take these threats seriously. I'd have to be a dummy not to. A dummy, or else as tough as Charles Bronson, which I assuredly am not. I never call the cops when I get one of these threats. I know what they'd probably say, "Leitner? So what?"

In order to motivate a death threat, you have to be making people uncomfortable by doing something a little different on their TV screen. Our weekend weatherman, Doug Oliver, once got a snake in the mail. Someone actually sent him a box with a small snake in it. I forget if it was a rattler or a garden snake, but the effect was the same. The newsroom cleared out in a hurry.

If this sort of thing isn't enough to make you a little dubious about the innate goodness of our species, I don't know what it would take. I mean, what could Doug possibly have done to deserve such treatment? Maybe he predicted clear weather and it rained instead. At any rate, I concluded that if Doug Oliver is going to get a rattler, some bozo will probably send me a python, one of those snakes as big as a football player's arm. My colleague, Jim Laslavic, reached a similar conclusion. He has a tendency to visit the Coke machine when I start opening my mail. Laz gets real nervous if he sees a box on my desk.

Laz is our latest Charger, and certainly the most competent on TV. Before we hired him, we used Dan Fouts and Hank Bauer as regular guests during the

21

season to provide some insight into the Chargers and their opponents. Kellen Winslow has been doing it for the last couple of years. I've tangled with all of them, just as I have with the common folk and the weirdos. We pay these guys for their insight, but too often we get clichés. For Fouts, coming to the studio and being on the air with me must have been like consorting with the enemy. And I think Bauer saw it much the same way. His objective seemed to be to try to show up "that idiot" Leitner. He would go to practice and brag about how he put me down. On the air, Hank acted like he hated me, even though he always assured me that wasn't the case.

Hiring Bauer was probably a mistake, because he really acted like a crazy man at times. I remember a Monday night when the Chargers were destroyed up in Seattle. The defense was just pathetic. Bauer came on the show with me the next day and just started raving. I asked him an innocuous little question, and he went berserk, right there in my office before a live camera. You couldn't see it on the screen at home, but the veins in his neck were bulging out like phone cords and he was red-faced and screamed at me. "Now look!" he yelled. "We're *tired* of all your criticism! And not just you, Ted. We're tired of all the fair-weather fans, too! We have three or four games left to play, and you have got to make up your mind right now. Either you're with us or against us. Make up your mind. And stop all this criticism."

I was sitting there, trying to be cool and calm, giving my little Mike Wallace nod, while a cautionary voice in my head was saying, "This guy is going to kick your butt. He's crazy."

After we wrapped up the segment and I threw it

back to Michael Tuck on the anchor desk, Bauer leaned over to me and asked, "You don't think I was too strong, do you?" "No, Hank," I replied, "that was standard humanoid behavior, if your knuckles happen to drag the ground, like Piltdown man."

The thing was, people loved Hank's act. The audience loves to see me put down because I'm usually up in my ivory tower giving athletes and the athletic establishment a hard time. The viewing public loved to see a guy like Bauer or Winslow assaulting me. They thought Bauer hated me for sure. After Charger home games, I did a radio call-in show from the stadium. They had me in this little glass booth, and people would walk by and glance at me like I was a condemned man. "Good luck with Hank tomorrow!" they'd smirk. They might have hated my guts, but they knew I had to deal with Bauer, and they couldn't keep from going, "Heh, heh, hope he doesn't rip you up too badly."

Winslow takes the opposite approach. Kellen works at coming across as Mr. Cool. He looks so detached as he sits there in front of the lockers reading his newspaper. He knows his teammates are watching, and it's as if he's saying he just doesn't want to deal with me. Never mind that he's getting paid $500 or $600 a week. His schtick is to ignore me, maybe I'll go away. He tries to be flip, so I just play along with it. That segment is pretty inane, anyway.

In the spring of 1985 I was offered a chance to be the play-by-play man on the Charger radio network. There are only 28 jobs like it in pro football, so I eagerly accepted. That doesn't mean I'm not going to be just as honest — critical, if need be — but it did mean I had to patch up a silly little feud I had with Rick Smith, the team's public relations man.

Rick's an old newspaper guy with a caustic sense of humor and a real antenna for what's said or written about the Chargers. If I say *anything*, in jest or in earnest, he's sure to hear about it. For years I'd take my shots, and I guess Rick must have been simmering the whole time. The ways he expressed himself were pretty funny — or juvenile, depending on your point of view.

For instance, to get back at me for something that made him angry, Rick didn't send me any press credentials for the 1984 season. It took me a couple of exhibition games to realize I hadn't received passes. I casually quizzed Laz, and learned he had his. "Rick told me you didn't get passes because you didn't make all the games last year," Laz told me. That struck me as a fairly dumb reason, since I was never aware that the Chargers were taking attendance in the press box. In reality, it was just Rick's way of getting around the real issue — that he was annoyed with me.

To be fair to Rick, in his official capacity he was just an extension of then owner, Gene Klein, who never understood or cared about the value of public relations. I believe the new owner, Alex Spanos, has a different attitude. He strikes me as a guy who can be tough and still be a man of his word. The players and media, and ultimately the fans, will benefit. I'm not saying Spanos doesn't have an ego. He does. I was told he once left his private box to go down to the field just so NBC could zoom in on his face for a brief shot, and then he rode the elevator back upstairs, satisfied with the return from his sweaty toy on that day.

I really believe the PR will improve under Spanos, and there won't be any more of the petty incidents that characterized my relationship with Smith. The funniest occurrence involved the Chargers' Christmas cheese box. The team had a policy of sending a gift of cheese to various members of the San Diego media. When mine didn't arrive, I talked about it on the Hudson and Bauer show.

"Guys, I'm crushed," I said. "I don't think the Chargers like me. They didn't send me my cheese."

The next day, it came. The address: "Big Mouth, Channel 8."

The Chargers' holiday spirit failed them again in 1984. No cheese for Ratso Leitner. Really, I could afford my own. But I wanted to have a little more fun with Hudson and Bauer.

"You dummy!" Mac Hudson said. "They didn't even send you any press credentials. You didn't really think they'd give you any cheese, did you?" And I thought, gee, it's fun to be seven years old again.

CHAPTER 4

The Fatal Attraction —
Athletes and Women

I don't understand women. Let me be more specific. I don't understand what they expect from me, in relation to my job as a sportscaster. And I don't completely understand what they see in ballplayers.

Once I was accosted in the parking lot of a Gemco store by a woman who came charging at me with a shopping cart. It was the wife of former Padre second baseman Juan Bonilla. As she came rushing at me behind the cart, I imagined the headlines: "Sportscaster hit by cart; in serious but stable condition." She slowed down before I died and was buried. Then, having drawn my attention, Mrs. Bonilla proceeded to deliver a lengthy harangue regarding some minor indiscretion I had committed in a recent commentary about her husband.

I got in trouble with the other side of the infield during spring training 1985, following a mildly critical commentary on third baseman Graig Nettles. About a half hour after I signed off, our producer came into my office and warned us that there was a woman named Ginger Nettles on the line, cursing and howling. She'd told him I had a vendetta against Graig and claimed I was out to get him in my New York style. Finally, the producer had gotten tired of listening and told her to call back and talk to Leitner.

I had done what I considered a playful open letter to Nettles, the thrust of which was, "Hey, Graig, relax." "You're going to be 41," I said. "Yet every time I turn around, another reporter is telling me how you turned down an interview. Come on, you're back home in San Diego. You're not in New York, with all that Billy Martin, George Steinbrenner crap to worry about. There are no hateful reporters hunting you down and making up negative stories. You're among friends here and you're getting a fair shake in the media."

I then cited an example of how a radio announcer had approached Graig for an interview during the stretch run for the pennant in September 1984. Nettles was lounging there with his feet up at his locker. "Nah," he said, "I'm too tired. Find someone else." Well, I'm sorry, Graig, that's bullshit. This was the Padres' network announcer requesting an interview for the post-game show. Beyond having an obligation to the Padres, a ballplayer has to realize it's good business sense to do these things. You go on radio, your name is spread, you get endorsement opportunities. So give your local radio guy five minutes. You get a free watch or something. If you don't need the watch, give it to a rookie making minimum salary. He'd be happy to get it.

I wasn't really being hard on Graig. But I wasn't exactly finished with him yet. I told the audience how Channel 8 had sent a reporter out to Yuma. "Graig, got a couple of minutes?" our man said. "Nah," he replied and walked away. Thanks, Graig.

Another radio producer was trying to do some Padre profiles for broadcast on KFMB. In return for a few minutes, he was offering a Watchman TV. Nettles seemed slightly interested and indicated he would do the interview in an hour. But when the time came, he declined.

My opinion of the man is, he thinks he's a bigshot future Hall of Famer. He's a witty guy when he wants to be, and he was a great talent. But there was just no reason for him to pull that New York stuff in San Diego. So I ended my commentary by suggesting he stop and smell the roses, because in a couple of years, nobody's going to care what he has to say, anyway. "Graig," I said, "you've been lucky. Blessed. How about returning some of that to baseball?"

I can give you another example of the legend-in-his-own-mind syndrome. Cecil Cooper of the Milwaukee Brewers announced he was not going to do any more interviews in 1985 because he didn't want the distraction. Distraction, huh? The great San Francisco columnist Herb Caen made the most telling point about the press on this score. "The sports press made you guys," Caen wrote once in addressing contemporary athletes. In the old days in pro football, they used to pass the hat to help make the payroll. And baseball, he noted, didn't just arrive on the scene and start drawing 40 million fans. In the old days, the sports writers were widely read and wielded great influence. Guys like Ring Lardner, Grantland Rice, and Heywood Hale Broun painted heroic portraits of Babe Ruth and other sports figures. The writers helped make the games what they are. But today's athletes don't need to be "distracted." Just let 'em collect their $1 million paychecks and their endorsements and their six months off, without giving anything back to the public.

The nerve — to call doing an interview a distraction! Just take the benefits and return nothing. Contemporary

Athletes give you that crap that as long as they give 100 per cent on the field, they're doing their job. Well, that's absolutely wrongheaded.

I had an argument with Padre catcher Terry Kennedy on this subject. Without radio, TV, and newspapers, I said, there's no way he would be making $700,000 a year. He wouldn't make half of that. The TV networks pay such big fees for the rights to show games, they foot a lot of the salary bill. Players definitely owe the media some of their time. The so-called distraction helps them make a helluva living. Without the media, the fans just would *not* be there in such numbers.

The players chose to work in a public profession with a history of media involvement. That's the way it is. Nettles could turn down a request from KFMB in spring training, but when the paperback edition of his book, *Balls* was published, he was more than willing to go on the same radio station to hype his project. That's the way the modern ballplayer thinks, and Graig Nettles is hardly the exception. But I just can't buy that mentality. There's no excuse for it. The players should be ashamed. If I owned a team, it would be stipulated in each player's contract that he would do everything reasonable to accommodate the media and to promote the team and the game.

The wives of the players seem to have an even bigger problem than the players do in understanding the role of the media. When you deal with the wives, there's a chill in the air. In their eyes if you're critical of their husbands, you're jeopardizing the job and the security of the family. I can understand their sensitivity. And, in truth, I never had any problem with Ginger Nettles until this spring. She waved to me in the lobby of the Padres' hotel at the World Series. Graig didn't even acknowledge me.

Wives, girl friends, or groupies, women love athletes. I must confess, I don't know what the attraction is. Ever meet a professional athlete? We're not talking brain surgeon IQs. I thought women had taste. I thought they liked suave, debonair guys with social graces who can read without moving their lips. Guys who know which salad fork to use. But, no! Women love athletes.

I have to figure it's just physical attraction. It can't be intellectual. But it's gotta be exciting for a woman to sit up in the stands and turn to a friend and say, "See No. 22 scratching his crotch? That's my boy friend." Wow! Then they get to stand outside the players' entrance and greet the boy friend.

It's Disneyland traveling with a team. I remember once flying into Chicago with the Padres. A player yelled out, "Get out your E coupons." And he wasn't referring to shopping. No, he meant Rush Street, where the girls are. Of course, they're also in the hotel lobbies, outside the locker rooms, all over.

Joe Pepitone went into specifics about ballplayers' away-from-home sex lives in his book *Joe, You Coulda Made Us Proud*. Some women just love athletes — wholesale. "Look up Joan in Atlanta," a guy may tell a teammate, "she does everybody." There are lots of Joans in every American city.

What it comes down to, I think, is that it's status for a woman to be seen with a player. Back when I worked in Philadelphia, I once went out to the airport to do a story on the Phillies clinching the pennant. There were all the wives standing in a group on the tarmac. Good Lord, I thought, look at those women. Bob Boone's wife and Dick Ruthven's, among others, were knockouts. And I thought, "Dammit, I know their husbands. A lot of them are very dull guys. If you spotted 'em the C and the A, they couldn't spell cat." And I looked at the ladies, intelligent, classy women. What is it that attracted them? Money. Ego. Status.

I know there are more hairdryers and drugs and money in pro sports these days, but one thing hasn't changed. The thing with the groupies. They were there in the day of Ruth and Gehrig, and they're here today. They have freer mores now, I guess. And, boy, am I jealous.

Some of the players are going to go for it, of course. There was a Padre player who came stumbling in one morning and called the front desk and said he wanted to have a wake-up call at 7:30 a.m. "I'm sorry, sir," the operator said. The guy started getting belligerent. "What do you mean? I'm a guest in this hotel. I want a wake-up call," he sputtered. Finally, the operator got in a word and said, "Sir, I would be happy to oblige, but it's already 8:15 in the morning."

One time at Atlanta Stadium, I was riding the press elevator with a woman who'd been with a Padre player the night before. She asked me if I knew who number such-and-such was. She didn't even know his name! Think of it. She had slept with this guy and didn't even know him except by number. I told her, of course, I know the guy. "Weeelll," she drawled, "thaaaat's my boy friend."

It's just fascinating to me that athletes are so sought after. You'd think women would be after super successful businessmen with high IQs. No — they want ballplayers. Guys who run fast and are endowed.

There's a great line about Willie Mays. Milton Berle said he heard how all these athletes are supposed to be endowed. He couldn't speak from firsthand knowledge, but he'd seen a picture in the paper, and he would guarantee Earl Scheib couldn't paint a son of a bitch like that for $29.95. It crosses all bounds, all races, colors, and creeds. Basketball, baseball and football. And, like I said, I'm jealous as hell. I'll give the players the enormous salaries. But I'll never forgive them for getting more and better women.

CHAPTER 5

The Gospel of Crapola

Loyalty is important to me. Loyalty to family, loyalty to job, and loyalty to my viewers. I hate to sound pompous, but that's how it is. I'm loyal to the truth, but not to the Padres, the Chargers, or any other team. I've worked on broadcasts where the teams had a say in the selection of the commentators, but I've never compromised my principles. I don't expect players to understand. Basically, I believe management understands — they just don't like it. They want you to shill and sell tickets. Management thinks you're hurting the club by telling the truth. Nonsense. You sell tickets if you have a sound product. Anybody who says I keep people from going to the stadium is crazy. I don't have that power or that intention.

The ballplayers are offended, naturally, by any hint of criticism. Their egos get in the way of objectivity. If I say a guy doesn't have good range, he isn't thinking of his next contract, he's thinking of his ego. The attitude is, "You never played ball, Leitner." It's like when a reviewer says a movie is bad — an actor will react by saying the reviewer never did any acting. I don't expect a player to like it when I'm critical, but there ought to be that rare individual who understands that I have a job to do and a right to report what I see. Terry Kennedy of the

Padres is one who seems able to see that. When he plays lousy, he admits it. But he's an exception.

It's not my job to be liked by the players. Show me a writer or sportscaster who's popular with the players, and I'll show you a guy who's kissing ass and not doing his job. He's not being honest.

Let me put it this way. I do want to be liked, but I won't do less than my best job just because I want Graig Nettles to like me. I won't spread the gospel of crapola. Dave Campbell, the Padres' color man, is the same way, and I respect him for it. He was a player, and he gets more grief than I do. He works for the ball club and he's still honest. He faces the flack, and I think that's terrific.

I respect a guy like baseball writer Barry Bloom of the *San Diego Tribune*, who criticizes players and knows he's got to walk into that clubhouse and try to get quotes the next day. He's got guts, and the players should respect that. Many just aren't intelligent enough to see it.

You might think there's commercial pressure from the sponsors. Let me tell you otherwise. If a person gets on the air and kisses the Chargers' tail, it's not because he's afraid of the sponsors of the show. He's more worried about what Coach Don Coryell may say. I'll give you another example. If an announcer refuses to talk about the offensive linemen the Chargers have been grooming, it's because the guy just doesn't want to face the players in question.

Too many sportscasters and sports writers aren't willing to offend anybody. They're just plain scared. And let me make a further point here. It's one thing to write an opinion in the newspaper. It's something else to get on TV and do it like you're talking face to face. It can be insulting, no doubt about it. It has more impact in living color.

Know what? It's like getting up at a party in somebody's living room and attacking the host. "You call these hors d'oeuvres! Look at this house! Look at the dirt on the carpet! Lousy food, lousy party, I'm outta here!" It's literally like that. And the consequences are tougher for broadcasters than for newspaper writers.

Tommy Nettles, the former Aztec wide receiver and a cousin of Graig, made a related discovery when he moved from doing radio commentary to television. He's a very honest, opinionated guy like me, but he couldn't do it on TV. He said he could give an opinion on radio, but not on TV. He couldn't even think of doing the same commentary on TV, because you're right out there saying it face to face.

I hadn't really thought of it in those terms until Tommy said it. But it's true. I may go on the air some night and say, "Don Coryell looks like a jerk on the sideline. Looks like somebody put Elmer's glue in his deodorant. He's got his arms hanging out and he's hitching up his pants. Does this guy know what's going on?" When I say something like that before God and country on TV, there's a pretty good chance somebody will see it and tell the coach about it.

This is as good a place as any to say that I'm not real proud of most sportscasters. In fact, there is a legacy of broadcasting sellouts. They've been in it to make money, and I understand that. A few guys like Edward R. Murrow and others at CBS News have taken a stand, but for the most part, they've just wanted to play it safe. The networks, bless 'em, would rather have a show like Hollywood Wives, the most incredible piece of crap ever on TV, than a controversial sportscast. They want to air revenue-maximizing stuff and stay away from any controversy that might irritate the sponsors.

Give credit to Howard Cosell. He was the first to go against the grain. He had no predecessors on radio or TV. Walter Winchell did some hard-hitting stuff, but he got a little too powerful and could destroy careers and lives.

In the 1920s and 1930s, the sponsors had nearly complete control over the content of radio programming, and the announcers had very little license. The reward for honesty was a pink slip. No one had ever heard of Nielsen ratings 40 years ago, but the pressure to please was there just the same.

As far as I know, no one in radio who ever dared go against the NFL. Nor anyone say that Babe Ruth was a womanizer and a drunk who ate like a pig. They didn't say that on the air, because it would have been seen as destroying a hero. It was no different with the newspapers. Sports writers turned out flowery prose, and some of it was pretty damn good. But it didn't touch the morals or the life style of the ballplayers. And that's the tradition I'm working against, a tradition of ass-kissers and hero worshippers, never getting anyone mad.

I guess it all began to change in the 1950s and 1960s. America seemed to lose its innocence. As the country began examining some of its closely held beliefs, the role of the media shifted. There was more interpretation and more analysis. Inevitably, more opinions were written and broadcast. I would like to think the media began to look at sports more realistically. The games were still important, but the media began looking for something more. The story behind what happened on the field. The private lives of the players. Suddenly, the fans were taken places they'd never been before. And they were pretty much compelled to rethink their attitudes toward sports.

The essential point I've always tried to make is that sports isn't serious. Just about everything I say on TV and radio follows from that one little assumption. Sports really isn't serious. It's a game.

There are some serious aspects of sports. Drug use. Racism. The big-business side of it. The hypocrisy. But I think we should see this and laugh and point out our foibles and double standards and become a better country. It ain't enough to be the best. If we can't poke fun and say, "This is only fun and games," we're in trouble. We just can't keep paying college players who are totally illiterate. We're Americans. We shouldn't do that.

When I was real young, I worked for a radio station in Cushing, Oklahoma. A little 200-watt station that broadcast only in the daytime. I did the games of the Cushing High Tigers. Armed with a flashlight and my Wollensak tape recorder, I described the game for broadcast the next morning. You can imagine how large the audience was. Couple of hundred farmers, I guess. But, man, did those people take their football seriously. And I learned a vitally important lesson. As I looked around during a timeout, I would see bankers and preachers screaming, the veins bulging out on their necks. They were cussing and using language that would make a 20-year Navy man blush.

I realized right then that oil isn't the biggest thing in Oklahoma. Football is. And the school system? It didn't mean much. I got a letter from a kid who wrote, "I heard you don't like the Sooners. I told them it wasn't so, it was just a roomer." Boomer Sooner Roomer. There was another letter. It began, "Now just a minet." It amazed me people would take sports so seriously, at the expense of the educational system. I don't know where they thought the next generation of petroleum engineers was going to come from.

Of course, we're not just talking Oklahoma here, folks. The same attitudes prevail in Baja Oklahoma, which is how the writer Dan Jenkins referred to the state of Texas. Maybe we shouldn't leave out Baja Oregon, either. Or *any* of the lower 48. We're talking about a national consensus.

It's a fact. The vandalism rate goes up after losses by local teams. The suicide rate, too. I'll be damned if I'll take any ball game that seriously. I want to have fun and be conversational. Yet some of my audience think I should be depressed if the Chargers don't go to the playoffs.

After the Pittsburgh Steelers won their fourth Super Bowl, their coach, Chuck Noll, walked into a restaurant and heard the maitre'd say, "I'm so thankful. You made me proud to be from Pittsburgh." Noll, an artist and a man who knows gourmet food, realizes football is his job, but it's not important in the overall scheme of things. He was struck by how this waiter seemed to be ashamed to be from Pittsburgh. But a winning team made him proud.

Philadelphians were the same way. I did some time in Philadelphia. Those good people actually believe those W. C. Fields jokes about the city of losers. It was like somebody calling them jerks or questioning their mother's morals. They believed their teams truly represented their city. I say, "Bull! How about your fire department? Or your police? The school system? But not the win-loss records of your teams." I'll be damned if I'll go for that.

When the Chargers play the Dallas Cowboys, it's us against them. And if the Chargers win, we're supposed to be better than Dallas. Sorry. To my way of thinking, if we had a better educational system than Dallas, that might mean something. But it wouldn't mean too much. I read that the billionaire H. Ross Perot said the Texas high school football system should be changed. The overemphasis on football was corrupting the academic process, he said. And he came up with a proposal that made sense. For a kid to be eligible to participate in football in the fall, he had to have passed all his work the previous semester. Some legislators got hold of the idea and extended it to other sports. The rationale was terribly simple: Get the school system up to the point where a graduate can actually spell and conjugate a verb.

The problem is so widespread, it's a national scandal, in my estimation, and I will not go along with hyping athletics for athletics' sake. Far too many kids who are shortchanged by the educational system because they can run 100 yards in less than ten seconds, or they can make a jumpshot from 20 feet. I'm supposed to go on the air and talk seriously about that kind of national disgrace? I'd resign and go into another business before doing that.

I make my living in sports, but I will not take it seriously. I just don't happen to like the idea of paying kids who can't spell to play basketball. There was some 6'9" guy from Creighton who was pictured several years ago when he went to class with little elementary school kids at their desks. I respected the guy for doing it. But the point is, he had done four years at Creighton and wasn't much closer to graduating than a two-year-old. I'm sure he realized what nonsense he was facing. He had to have felt used. He didn't have his eligibility and his jump shot anymore, and he couldn't read or write.

And how many more are there out there? How many Chris Washburns are there? You remember Washburn. He was the North Carolina State freshman who made a ridiculously low score on his college admission test, but was accepted anyway.

I know what the reaction to this will be. "You better shut your mouth, Leitner." I expect a reaction when I say things like this. But I've got to do it. And I'm lucky, really, because I have an outlet.

Lots of people who call me on talk shows are irate about something. The Chargers raised ticket prices and they want to cancel their tickets. I hear what they're saying, and I get upset and rant and rave. People enjoy listening because they don't have a forum like mine. And it's my responsibility to use it, unlike people on other channels, who think they just have to keep the Chargers and Padres happy.

I owe my audience more. I know they get mad. And I want to get it off my chest on their behalf.

I know that if people didn't take sports seriously, I wouldn't be making good money. In effect, I am not just hitting the golden goose, I'm talking about a kick in the groin. It's like guys in dentistry trying to find a vaccine to prevent tooth decay. They might just put themselves out of business.

If the day comes when fans no longer call up and bitch because the ticket prices were raised, then I'm in trouble. If everything was wonderful, I might be out of a job. But I have a feeling it's just me letting off steam, and I don't really change anybody's thinking. I know full well they do take sports seriously. I am not naive or egotistical enough to believe I can change what people think, in any large way.

There's not a lot of sermonizing in this book. But if you're going to understand me, it's important to know that I'm an idealist. I always have been. I look at the trillions of dollars spent since World War II on defense. And I look at Reagan's budget. And then I see welfare programs cut and Social Security programs frozen, all for bombs and bullets. Is this necessary? All because governments can't get along. If they didn't have to threaten each other and not get along, I'm convinced we would have a cure for cancer and heart disease by now. My God, why can't we use our riches for something constructive?

I'm stupid enough to believe it's a possibility. Well, not really. But wouldn't it be wonderful. One people, one earth, like the bumper stickers say.

Let me get in a word about organized religion, and then we'll get back to the heavy stuff, I promise. There is no more divisive force than organized religion. That's the one thing I have against religion. It may give people faith and strength. But for all the good it does, it's done so much harm. Because Moslems are convinced they gotta kill Christians. And Jews. If God is watching, he's going to see a lot of people who are blowing it, killing in his name. It just makes me crazy to see someone in Iran being shot because of a different religious or sexual preference. How can people get mad about the sports tripe I deal in?

I remember when the Ayatollah seized power. He withdrew Iran's wrestling team from some tournament. I went on the air and said, "What are we going to do without the Iranians? They have two national sports — wrestling and executions." The Iranians at United States International University were just thrilled when I said that. I was *real* popular with them. I'm sure they loved it when I added, "I wonder if Iranian TV has any Howard Cosells to do play-by-play of executions?"

It's like I said. Sports isn't serious.

CHAPTER 6

To Have and Have Not

I'm always getting ripped for dwelling on the subject of money. I confess, I like the stuff. And I defy anyone to name a better common denominator for the sports fan and the athlete. I defy anyone to come up with a bigger continuing story in the realm of sports. I can't talk about drugs all the time. But I can talk money. It's mind-boggling. Each new contract seems to outdo the last. A couple of years ago George Foster signed a contract with the Mets for a $1 million cash bonus, plus a limousine to pick him up at his penthouse and transport him to the playground in Queens. Oh, yeah, they threw in a $2 million salary. Now if this sort of detail doesn't fascinate you, my guess would be you don't have a pulse.

I just don't think you can talk about money too much. Try to check out of the supermarket by telling them money isn't important. I've already made the point that athletes tend to be dumb, but they're not dumb enough to refuse when someone offers a vault full of cash. Jackie Gleason once said nobody is overpaid, and I agree, in a sense. If some guy is willing to sign the check, take it.

From my perspective, it doesn't make much sense socially to pay a shortstop $2 million and pay a cop

$25,000. But I always get an argument when I challenge the established values of our society.

I'm fascinated by the subject of money. Always have been. I grew up without it, like so many jocks, and I don't ever want to be without it again. When I was growing up, if one of my brothers or I left a light on in the apartment, that was a mortal sin. A guaranteed spanking. We could be outside playing stickball and Dad would yell, "Come up here!" You would come running, thinking it was going to be something important. And he would confront you with the question, "Why is this light on?" Sometimes I would play the wiseass and say, "Gee, Dad, I don't know. Maybe it's on because there's electrical current flowing. Don't ask me, ask Thomas Edison. I don't know the laws of thermodynamics." I would give an answer like that, then I would duck. And reach for the light switch.

The entire time I was growing up, we lived in a two-bedroom apartment in Yonkers, New York. There was a living room, a kitchen and two bedrooms. My parents slept on a fold-out sofa in the living room. My older brother had one bedroom, and my younger brother and I shared the other bedroom.

I got a terrific education in the value of the dollar, and I've never lost interest. I have been thinking of buying a white Ferrari, which I've wanted for a long time. It would be a great contrast to the cars of my youth. My Dad was the only guy I ever heard of who always bought a car without a radio. He even managed to find the model with no arm rests in the back seat. There were vinyl seats that stuck to your rear end. If he hadn't smoked, I doubt that he would have taken the cigarette lighter.

To say we lived a Spartan existence would be an

understatement. There was no carpeting in the apartment. Just bare linoleum floors. It was a shock on a winter morning when the bare soles of your feet made contact with the linoleum. The temperature of the floor was always around absolute zero because of the inefficiency of our radiators. You could touch the surface without burning your fingertip.

I enjoy dressing nicely now, so long as I keep my weight down and feel I deserve to wear expensive clothes. I went three years without buying any nice things for myself because I was 40 pounds too heavy. I could afford things, but I just wouldn't reward myself.

It wasn't like that when I was a kid. My senior year of high school, I had one pair of pants. They were like Henry Ford's old car: any color you want, so long as it's black. I wore those pants every day, and the seat got so shiny it must have glowed in the dark. I could be seen at night by passing motorists.

Along with the black trousers, I had white socks, a pair of brown loafers and several shirts. One was was red, another pastel, the third was purple. I would roll up the sleeves, like a hoodlum. Except I didn't stick a pack of cigarettes in the sleeve.

It always amuses me to read the interviews with athletes in the papers. They sign a fat contract and buy a big house and all the goodies that go with it, and then they get around to telling what they wanted as a kid and were denied.

My passion? White bucks. Like Pat Boone and Elvis Presley wore. I wanted them so badly. If someone had offered me white bucks for having my left foot amputated, I would have shouted, "Start sawing, Kildare!" I would have gladly hobbled around in one white buck.

In those days (the late 1950s), a pair of bucks went for about five dollars. I never got 'em.

I also yearned for a guitar. I was wearing my hair like Presley, and I wanted to strum the guitar the way he did. Man, I wanted to take lessons and learn to play. Naturally, Dad would have no part of that idea. Who knows, I might have been bigger than Michael Jackson.

The point is, I grew up not having much, and I just accepted being turned down when I asked for something. Eventually I just stopped requesting.

I have a pool in my backyard now, but I never would have dreamed of that as a kid. In the first 18 years of my life, I never even visited a house with a pool. Heck, I rarely set foot in a house, period. We had an apartment, as did everyone we knew. The first house I ever lived in, I bought.

If I seem fascinated with money, it's because I like what it can do for you. It can give you independence or luxury, as you choose. Some people are given to extravagance, but I'm not one of them. A $50 bill is still big money to me. I have respect for money, never having had any in my early years.

When I finished college and started work in Oklahoma City in 1972, my beginning salary was $7,800. I thought if I ever got to $10,000, there would be nothing more I could want. This was before heavy inflation. For $30,000 you could buy a heckuva house in Oklahoma City.

It's easy for me to identify with ballplayers who come into pro sports and blow a lot of money. They don't have the education or the background to handle big money. They buy clothes, cars, drugs, what have you, and some wind up with nothing. It's easy for me to understand how someone who's never had to practice restraint could go absolutely crazy with the money that suddenly becomes available.

I've come to really appreciate money. I want my kids to have more than I had. Forgive me if I sound like a child of the Depression. I want my kids to have it all, but I don't want to spoil them. That's the great paradox of twentieth century American materialism, I suppose. My kids never will know what it's like to be without. They'll never be hungry. They'll never want white bucks *soooo* bad, because I will just buy them. Maybe I — and thousands of parents like me — are doing the kids a disservice. If anyone who reads this can offer some expert guidance, I would like to hear it.

I appreciate money, and I truly appreciate the house it has enabled me to buy. To this day I walk into my home and if I'm alone, I'll say to myself, "I like this place." Sure, the kids take it for granted. But I don't.

My brother and I used to save our money so we could buy tickets to sit in the bleachers at Yankee Stadium to see the football Giants. I asked my son last year, when he was ten, if he wanted to go to a Charger game. "Sure, Dad," he said. "Who's playing?" At that moment I realized I had created a monster. The kid had to ask who was playing, as if it mattered to a ten-year-old. If the Chargers aren't playing the Dallas Cowboys, the boy doesn't want to go. I mean, he's been to Olympic Stadium in Montreal, Shea Stadium in New York, Busch Stadium in St. Louis. He takes it all for granted. Christmas comes and I buy him $300 worth of presents. If you added up the value of all the presents I received in my life, it wouldn't total $300. He's got 75,000 toys, so naturally he takes it for granted.

Given the choice, I guess I would have enjoyed being spoiled as a kid. Who am I kidding? Of course, I would have.

Yet it gave me pause when a neighbor told me one day that when he was 15 minutes late picking up his kids at school, his son asked where he had been. I could not conceive of asking my Dad why he might have been late for anything. I would have trudged to algebra in snow drifts up to my behind for the rest of the year. I could have got frostbite, he wouldn't have softened. If I shot my mouth off, I walked.

There's something paradoxical in what I'm about to say, I suppose, but I've turned down million-dollar jobs in New York. Maybe I've matured. The point is, I'm established here, I'm having fun, and I'm near my kids. I like the variety of what I am doing, and I simply wouldn't leave solely to make more money. Of course, if I got an overwhelming network offer, I would have to consider that. I have commuted to see my kids before, and I could do it again. But in terms of the job, I don't need the number one market to feed my ego.

I have started over several times, competing against guys who were long accepted in people's living rooms, and it's no picnic. I came to realize the older guys who stayed put in one market were not so dumb after all. Guys like Bob Dale and Ray Wilson. They knew what they were doing in not moving just for the sake of the ego and the dollar. I'm sure they don't see themselves as failures, and I don't either. They maintained their rheostats at acceptable levels, and I'm learning to do it. I know what's out there, and I know I could make it. But I wouldn't leave San Diego just to be in a larger market and have a few more expensive toys.

CHAPTER 7

Freshness Is All

Whatever our line of work, we all need to think we're doing it the right way. If we're talented, we think we're doing it the best way. When I get criticized by a rival, I have to weigh it against my own standards and beliefs. One of my competitors, Mike Smith of Channel 10, boasts of taking four and a half hours to prepare for a sportscast. The implication is that I just wing it, with no preparation. Well, after 15 years in the business, I wouldn't be bragging about it if I needed half the day to get ready.

One of the tired old criticisms of Leitner is that there aren't enough scores on my show. Hey, I give the rudimentary scores, baseball, football, basketball. If I don't give the complete hockey scores, that's mainly because of a shortage of time. Let's say it's mid-October, when baseball is hot and basketball is starting and the NFL is revved up. Who wants all the scores from the Smythe Division and the Campbell Conference? There can't be that many people in the San Diego audience waiting up until 11 p.m. to get the Vancouver Canucks–Chicago Black Hawks score, right? To give all those scores, plus the tennis from Bangkok and Rangoon, it's just too boring. I get three minutes, and I'll be damned if I am going to spend it boring people with stuff that's gonna be formatted much more legibly in the newspaper the next day.

Uh, oh. Here comes that word. Entertaining. But let me qualify it to make myself feel better. I want to have an entertaining sportscast. It always kills me when a guy like Gus Stevens, who calls himself a critic for the *San Diego Tribune*, gets on me. I'm not even convinced Stevens owns a TV, based on what he writes. He puts it in terms of, well, Leitner is not a sportscaster, he's an entertainer. First of all, when did it have to be totally separated? How about being an entertaining sportscaster?

I estimate people are watching an hour of local news, or in Los Angeles, three hours of local news. If you're going to make people watch all that stuff, can't some of it be lighter than serial murders, gang rapes, Afghanistan, and bunches of heavily armed morons raising havoc? Can't we periodically show some funny footage of millionaire jocks falling down on the football field, or baseball players dropping the ball? Sometimes the pros look as human as you and me.

Some of these guys who criticize me for leaving out the scores not only work from a script, but they also tape a narration of almost every piece of footage in advance. When they go to the Padre highlights, they also hit a tape they recorded three hours ago. Many of them don't even trust their ability to ad lib for live narration. There are guys in this market who have done that for years. They say, "Oh, I could ad lib, but I would rather not." OK, fine. Then let's see you do it, fellows.

I work at being spontaneous. I want to just go in there, do my best, and see what happens. When people sit around and talk — a form of free association — they often come up with something new or different. That's my approach. No way do I want to sit down and write out a script. I can't sit there and say, gimme a funny line. You won't be funny or good that way. The fun for me is in being spontaneous.

I don't want to create the wrong impression here. I do a lot of homework. I look through all the wire copy that comes into the office. But long before that, I'm at home reading. The *New York* and *Los Angeles Times*, the *San Diego Union* and *Tribune*, *USA Today*, *Sports Illustrated*, *Inside Sports*, *Baseball Digest*, plus all the tripe and releases from all the commissioners' offices. It all goes into my head.

I seem to remember most of this stuff I read. For example, I just came across an anecdote about basketball coach Bill Fitch. He got mad and was thrown out of a game. Before leaving the floor, he grabbed the referee's whistle and took it with him to the locker room. I remember that and try to use it in a spontaneous situation.

If I hear a good story at a banquet, I may borrow it. It's OK to steal, if you steal funny stuff. The comedian Maury Amsterdam, who was on the old Dick Van Dyke Show, did books full of thousands of jokes he'd heard, and he can remember them all. To protect himself, he writes them down, so he has a joke for every situation or topic. Bob Hope has a vault full of his jokes. That material is his life. In case you're wondering, I have no vaults full of jokes. Nor money.

My desire to be spontaneous has its origins in my childhood, in the days before teleprompters. I'd sit there watching TV, with the newscaster's head going up and down as he read from his script. One time I saw a guy do a promotional announcement, and he had to look down for the call letters of his station. I like to look and sound fresh, not like some mechanical man without a thought in his head.

The big thing now is reading the teleprompter. You can see a newscaster's eyes moving, almost imperceptibly. The eyes are following the line. Very few are so good you can't pick up the movement. Take Jim Lampley of ABC. His eyes seem to go straight out, making eye contact. It's like he's saying, "They're going to think I'm brilliant. They won't know I'm reading." Well, too bad, Jim. Hate to give you away.

In addition to looking as natural as possible, I also like to speak naturally, and avoid talking like no sports fan in the entire universe ever talked. You know what I mean. "The Aztecs got nipped. The Padres were edged." That stuff may be fine for print, but in terms of TV, well, you never heard Eric Sevareid talking about how the Russians got edged and nipped. Fans don't sit around in bars and argue why the Padres were edged last night, do they? I don't want to sound that way, and I don't want to look that way, with my head bobbing up and down.

When I was beginning in this business, I admit, I tried to memorize a script. But then I realized, the people have their own newspapers, and they don't need me to read the news to 'em. At that stage of my career, I went to an outline, arranging topics in the order I wanted to proceed, leading up to my commentary. The big change for me came in 1976, when I was about to leave Hartford and move to Philadelphia. My idea was, as a lameduck announcer, to put aside the outline and go cold turkey. That was when I decided to be fresh, spontaneous. I haven't changed since. I have my stories in order, so the producer will be able to orchestrate the visuals, but beyond this I don't plan my delivery.

I consider it the highest praise when someone says I'm just talking to him or her in a conversational tone.

That tells me I'm communicating, not sounding like a guy reading a teleprompter. I like to think I'm just talking to the guy in front of his TV. It's something that just came about. Some people never get comfortable with doing it this way. I happen to love it.

I also look forward to broadcasting a ball game. The stadium is filling and you're ready to go on the air. Two minutes, one minute. That's what it's all about. I feel like I'm high. They do these studies about joggers who have endorphins released in the brain. I get that during and before a live broadcast of a game.

The highest I ever got was doing football — Aztec football play-by-play. I guess that makes me sound like an adrenalin junkie. I'd do the spotting charts and know the number of every player. I wouldn't need a spotter, because I was so ready. The quarterback gives the ball to a guy and I know his name, it comes right out, and that's a high. I've never actually done drugs, but I can't believe the experience would be any better than a live broadcast. That is one reason I look forward to doing Charger games on radio.

A conversational style is valuable to me, and I have confidence in it. The confidence can be a problem, though. The confidence can go at anytime. It went in Philadelphia. Back in Oklahoma City, I was starting to get good, and then I went to Hartford and became real good. I was different from anything else they'd ever had in that town. I was accepted and popular. I could not have lost that job in Hartford if I'd gone up to the news director's wife and jumped her bones. I was that confident I had the job.

Then the assistant news director from a Philadelphia station called me and said, "Hey, Leitner, you're offbeat. We'd love you in Philadelphia." I took the job, but within six months all that confidence was gone. I'll save the details for later. The important thing is that now I have confidence again, but I know it can go any moment. It's the same with any athlete or performer. Suddenly it just goes. They keep telling you that you're good and you don't believe it.

The realization I needed to be conversational and have fun at this job came before the confidence. I worked at being relaxed, realizing the camera was just a little lens with a red light on it. Relax, I told myself. And it worked.

The heartbeat still speeds up, of course. It's an old response from the cave days, rooted in the endocrine system. I can't stop it. I've been a guest speaker at General Dynamics with 1500 people in the audience. I'm sitting there after dinner and they're introducing me, and everyone starts looking at me. And then I walk up to the podium and I'm in the spotlight, and I'm ad libbing, and people are laughing. I'm totally confident at that moment. I look forward to it for weeks in advance.

If you put an EKG on me when I'm performing, you'd see my heartbeat is racing. I wouldn't be human otherwise. But there's a difference between the adrenalin flow from the excitement of performing and saying, "Oh, God, I'm going to wet my pants 'cause I'm so scared." I don't have that. I have the confidence of being established. I guess if I went to Los Angeles, where they don't know me, and it's a totally different audience, I'd be thinking differently. I don't assume I've got the whole business mastered. I don't.

Not everyone is going to be comfortable, of course. It's kind of like being a rabbit frozen in a truck's headlights. I'm not sure anybody ever gets comfortable unless they perform on a regular basis. You have to overcome that fear or you turn into a Freddie Prinze and blow your brains out.

The average businessman who goes to a sales seminar in St. Louis and is called upon for a presentation isn't going to be comfortable. It's like flying. The only way to get comfortable is to fly a lot. Go through a lot of different circumstances, turbulence, storms, bad landings. If you live through it, it comes easier. The guy who works at the grocery store and has to speak to a group of sales clerks is going to be scared to death. He isn't going to be able to look at it as I do and say, "Hey, this is fun."

But for all the fun and the highs, I can't say I had it all plotted out as a kid. That I ever got to this point seems like a major accident, if you want to know the truth. I never dreamed of going into TV until late in my high school years.

I played football for a couple years in high school, and I was pretty good at it. After my junior year, Joe Seidell, the athletic director, asked me if I'd like to announce the school basketball games. I don't know why he asked me. I was just sitting in the gym watching practice one day, because it beat studying.

The idea of doing something that required me to speak out in front of a group was quite radical. I was very shy in those days. In English or speech class, when they got to the L's, I'd play hooky. I would develop a sore throat the day before. But for some obscure reason, I heard myself saying yes to Coach Seidell, and I had myself a job announcing high school basketball.

My style was adopted from John Condon, the public address man at Madison Square Garden. I don't know if anyone could even hear me over our PA system, which was the equivalent of two juice cans on a string.

I liked it from the start. I decided quickly what I would do with my life. Despite never having been inside a radio or TV station, I made up my mind to go into broadcasting. Up to this point, I'd been planning to be a chemist, or an FBI man. You know how kids talk about those things without understanding what they're saying.

When I told Dad I planned to go into broadcasting, he said I ought to become a teacher and get steady work, like my older brother, who had enrolled at Oklahoma State. Tuition was low and state loans were available. Dad's attitude is understandable in retrospect. He grew up during the Depression, when the attitude was, get a steady job, don't gamble or try to be the best you can. Dad followed his own advice and was miserable all his life.

I followed my brother west and entered Oklahoma State in the fall of 1965. I knew I wanted to major in radio/television, but I also had secret designs on playing a little football.

I saw myself as a good player, and I *was*, in the context of the Yonkers public school system. As a junior, in spite of bad eyesight, I excelled as a split end. I remember a late afternoon game in autumn, no lights in the stadium, and in near darkness I caught a TD pass at the final gun. We won 7–6. Then my eyes got worse, and every game was like playing in Lincoln Tunnel at dusk.

On varsity squad at the start of my senior year, I couldn't even see the ball. I was elected co-captain, but the damn ball was a blur. I couldn't even see the laces. Nobody wore glasses inside the helmet in those days, so owing to my dimming vision, they shifted me to defense late in the season. I was real strong and I'd hit anything that moved.

Once I got to Oklahoma State in Stillwater, however, it didn't take long for the field to disabuse me of any illusions of a pro football career. Nobody warned me. I watched the varsity practice and discovered the missing element in my repertoire – quickness. Head Coach Phil Cutchen was a Bear Bryant disciple, and he wanted small, fast, quick, white linemen, 6 feet even and 185 pounds. I met half the requirements, white and 185. But I was just too slow. I knew I couldn't make the cut.

After watching one practice, I attended an orientation meeting with the head of the radio/TV department, Bob Lacey. He was to have a tremendous influence on me. When he asked me if I wanted to do play-by-play on the campus radio station, I jumped at the chance.

The varsity season opened a week later at Memorial Stadium in Little Rock, Arkansas. My colleague Steve O'Neal and I drove from Stillwater to what would be the first college game I ever saw. Fifty thousand fans were rocking the stadium, yelling "Soooooooeeeee!" It was like a religious revival meeting.

I announced the second half after doing color in the first half, pretending I was Paul Christmas or Al DeRogatis, stars on NBC at the time. I don't remember how nervous I was, but I must have been *very* nervous. We had no spotter and no statistician. I had no binoculars and couldn't even see the ball carriers. I wish I had a tape of that first broadcast. I'd love to play it on Hudson and Bauer and really get some belly laughs. I mean, I had a terrible New York accent.

It was a great opportunity to misbehave. You could only get the campus station at 660 AM in the dorms. If you were walking along the street and listening to a portable radio, you couldn't pick it up. The games were also broadcast on the main Oklahoma State network, so nobody listened to the campus station. Every time I stepped into a press box I pretended I was in the big time, with pregame meals, and major writers and broadcasters. What an education! I learned by doing.

I guess I backed into this career, but I have no regrets. I started doing daily sports shows on radio, and serving as a deejay. I made my share of mistakes. One time I was on the air with my foul New York mouth. I turned on my mike and started a record but accidentally left the mike on. When my program director walked in, I asked, "Why can't I hear this son of a bitch?" The director thoughtfully turned off the mike switch and advised me always to assume the mike is on.

It took several more knocks to finally shut me up. In one game, Oklahoma State was playing San Diego State, there was a fourth down, and Glenn Baxter of SDSU was punting. Out of my colleague's mouth came the phrase, "It's a 50-yard cunt by Baxter." I was in shock. The guys in the booth started to cough and laugh, and then the engineer stood up, smashing a light bulb above his head.

Much later in my career, on a Padre broadcast at Dodger Stadium, I was trying to phone my ex-wife from the press box to negotiate a visit with my son for the week. As Bob Chandler did the play by play, I took my earphones off but left my microphone on. I kept getting busy signals, so when I finally got through, I was irritated. Bob was on the air as I shouted, "What the hell. Were you talking to your broker?" Bob just chuckled. He knew it could have been worse, because in unguarded moments I talk like a New York street urchin. I hope I learn my lesson before it ends my career.

CHAPTER 8

The Comfort Barrier

Finding a style that works is important for every on-air person, but it doesn't happen overnight. It was the furthest thing from my mind as I approached the end of my college days. Survival was my number one priority. This was during the height of the Vietnam war, and I was fearful of being drafted. To be honest I dodged the draft by joining the National Guard. I was and am very patriotic, but the way I looked at it, I had spent four years in college doing nothing but working while other kids were enjoying their extracurricular activities. I didn't want to waste all the practical experience I'd acquired by working so many part-time jobs.

In the summers I worked for a little radio station in Wellington, Kansas, announcing Little League baseball games for $10 a night. I was earning $90 a week serving as a disk jockey in the afternoons, after which I would get in my car, grab a burger, and drive an hour to wherever the local team was playing. It might be 100 degrees, and the road through the wheat fields would be bumpy and dusty, and the smell of the fertilizer would be overpowering. The games might last three hours, because those kids were always throwing the ball away while their parents dozed in their lawn chairs and the score

mounted to 18–13, or something. I also did girls' soft-
ball, which was just as laborious.

During the regular school year, I also worked for
the campus radio station and stayed very busy, with this
and a full course load. I earned a 2.8 grade-point
average overall and made the dean's list several times.
Rather than waste all the effort I had put into my education, I decided to join the Guard. I served 4½ months of
active duty at Fort Polk, Louisiana, then returned to
Norman, Oklahoma, to work on a master's degree.
While I pursued the master's, I worked weekends as the
sports guy on Channel 9 in Oklahoma City, then got the
fulltime job as their sports director in 1972.

I never set out to be the next Howard Cosell, but it
didn't take me very long to start moving in that direction. Without the precedent Howard set, there is no way
anyone would want to watch me on television, let alone
read this book. I went through a certain amount of
trauma in Oklahoma City, and later in Hartford, because no one in those towns had ever done anything but
give the scores and conduct a few interviews.

The first time I really let it hang out was when I was
serving as the color man on the University of Oklahoma
football network. It was at a time when Mike Thomas,
who later played for the Chargers, had left the
Oklahoma squad in the aftermath of a fight with an
assistant coach. He happened to be leading the nation in
rushing at that juncture, so he was a valuable man. CBS
did a piece on the incident, and I put it on my show in
Oklahoma City with a little preface in which I alluded
to Thomas's differences with the staff. We did this piece
on the ten o'clock news, and the next morning I got a
call before eight o'clock from an irate Barry Switzer, the
head coach. I didn't even recognize his voice at first,

but it didn't take me long to figure out who it was. He argued I shouldn't have broadcast anything that was critical of Oklahoma football, to which I replied, "Barry, it's news. It affects Oklahoma." I've held that same basic conversation innumerable times since with other coaches. They expect that, since you're part of the broadcast team on game day, you'll be loyal and pay homage at every opportunity. The truth is, what I put on my daily TV show has nothing to do with what I say when I'm being paid by a team to do color commentary. But they're reluctant to acknowledge that point.

When I moved on to Hartford, I got into a controversy concerning fitness. I did a piece on large companies putting in gyms so employees could work out at lunchtime. One of the first groups to do so was one of the gigantic Hartford-based insurance companies. I went on the air and said, "Now why would an insurance company want its employees and other people to live longer? Gee, it's so selfless on their part, it shows so much concern. I'm really impressed." Of course, what I was implying was that the insurance company didn't want to pay off early on a policy, so they were trying to save some money by helping people live longer. Well, you could almost see the mushroom cloud roiling up on the horizon as I was finishing my commentary. The insurance companies didn't like it one bit. There were some high-level exchanges of fire, but my company backed me. Fortunately, the owner of the station had a sense of humor.

I ran into this sort of thing again when I moved on to Philadelphia. If I had a smile on my face when I came on the air, Philadelphians assumed I was a homosexual and a communist. I found out later through a friend that the Paley family, who founded CBS, watched my show in Philadelphia, and that they didn't like me at all. I was told the Paleys had decreed I wasn't good for the station and that I would have to go, which I did after a year.

While I was feeling my way along in this business, I discovered what a basically conservative country we live in. It's been conservative through its history in terms of dress, sexual mores, the influence of the church. The old-time smalltown press refrained from exposing a mayor who was stealing money or screwing around with another woman. They didn't cover the sweetheart land deal that involved a mayor who was getting rich because his brother was in real estate. You played ball. You went along. I came up against those tendencies time and again. You keep the power brokers happy.

This was where Cosell fit in, and this was where I picked up his lead. He wasn't some guy with a plastic pompadour like your typical news anchor. He had a voice that sounded like fingernails on a blackboard, but he made it on knowledge and confidence. His whole act was based on knowledge. We're talking about an educated man with a law degree and a photographic mind. The writer Larry Merchant once said Howard looked like the national poster boy for birth control. But he had a mastery of his material and great confidence, and no one could deny the basic validity of what he said.

Cosell lit up the switchboard at ABC by taking advantage of the fact that sports fans like to argue. Who's better — Willie Mays or Mickey Mantle? The Dodgers or the Yankees? Cosell was different, with his dark suit and his manner of Eric Sevareid, Jr. No one could figure where he fit in, because he got the fans involved, and no sportscaster had ever done it that way before. The fans got heated, and sometimes they wanted to kill him.

In a *Playboy* interview, Roone Arledge, the former head of ABC Sports and now in charge of its news division, told a story that pretty well captures the essence of how viewers related to Howard. It seems there was a bar near Denver where, every Friday night, the patrons would draw straws. The guy with the short straw would have to buy a black and white TV, while the fellow with the long straw would have the privilege of bringing his shotgun to the bar the following Monday. Against a backdrop of catcalls and screaming, the patrons could barely hear the words, "It's *ABC Monday Night Football* with Howard Cosell." And when Howard's face appeared, the guy with the gun would take aim and blow the hell out of that TV, and the joint would go crazy. Arledge said he was afraid that story would be very depressing to Cosell.

I'll tell you what's depressing to me. It's visiting Los Angeles and listening to *Dodger Talk* on KABC radio. There are homers. There are downright disgraceful honkers. But the industry standard has been set by *Dodger Talk*. It's the Hall of Fame homer program, the kind that would sicken Howard Cosell, and that sickens me, as well.

Have you ever *listened* to this incredible farce? If the Dodgers hired three people from their public relations department to anchor this turkey, it couldn't produce a more tasteless, rah-rah, Dodger propaganda. It's all in the same Dodger-blue vein. "So, we've lost 300 games in a row and we have no defense, but I just know we're going to win the pennant." If a little objectivity crawled into this show, it would immediately die of loneliness.

One of the hosts is Bud Furillo, a former newspaper columnist and a guy who had a reputation as being pretty darn objective. Now he's a broadcaster, and, in my opinion, somewhat less than objective. Sportswriters are constantly criticizing announcers for promoting, but one of their own has become the biggest honker who ever sat behind a microphone.

A couple of years ago, after the Padres swept the Dodgers four straight in San Diego, I started a campaign against the Dodger Crybabies. They complained about the Padres' supposed lack of etiquette in high-fiving and celebrating to excess. I had a lot of fun with the routine, and I got good mileage out of it. On the Dodgers' next trip to San Diego, they fared considerably better, and Dusty Baker devoted a portion of a postgame interview to me! "I hope Ted Leitner is happy now," Baker said. "I'd really like to thank Leitner for motivating us to win this series. I think the Padres should be real unhappy with Leitner for getting us up for this series." Thanks, Dusty. The Padres don't need any help finding things to be unhappy with me about, as we have already seen.

The Crybaby routine was about as much fun as I've had, and it went back to my habit of being a little different, a little more caustic than most of my colleagues. I don't know why, but the Crybaby thing seemed to irritate Vin Scully, the voice of the Dodgers. He used to say "hi" whenever we passed in the press box, but now we just look straight ahead and pass without speaking.

God, if I'd had an agent or manager, he would have been in heaven listening to all the promotion I received from the Crybaby thing. You couldn't buy that kind of publicity. So it was well worth losing an occasional "hi there" from Vin Scully. But make no mistake. Scully is the best there is in this business. A gentleman, a talent, a fine father, a man I envy and respect. Here's a guy everyone loves. He's supposedly getting $1 million a year from the Dodgers and another $1 million from NBC. What more could you want?

Go to a game at Dodger Stadium and the only thing you hear is Vin Scully. The fans bring their transistor radios to listen to him, and the Dodger broadcast is piped in to the concession stands. Scully's voice surrounds you. It's like the voice of God permeating Dodger Stadium. A few years ago, Vin was doing a game, and one of the game's umpires happened to be observing his birthday. Scully said that on the count of three, everyone should yell, "Happy birthday, Ed!" And 50,000 voices yelled "happy birthday" in unison. Unreal.

If I may be permitted one small criticism. Vin for years has violated one of the main tenets of the business. He talks too much. It's a three-hour talk show when Vin is on the air. Some of the lesser lights in my business get zapped for too much yapping, yet the guy who is considered the very best talks more than anyone else. For all the adulation of Scully, I haven't figured why nobody calls him for talking so much.

While Vin is the acknowledged best there is at baseball, I want to make a case here for Lindsey Nelson as the number one announcer in football. He is, hands down, the finest play-by-play football announcer who ever lived. Voice, pitch, balance, technique, accuracy, you name it, he's got it. I don't have any idea why CBS has relegated him to a relatively low position in the hierarchy. Pat Summerall can't even carry his microphone.

As long as we're discussing industry standards — guys you can't go wrong to emulate if you're a young broadcaster — the best in basketball is Chick Hearn. So maybe he's a little too Hollywood and too much in the Lakers' corner. Still, he's exciting, accurate, and knowledgeable. And he shows up for the job every day.

How many decades has it been since he missed a Laker broadcast? In spite of being a Laker employee, he gets pretty damn good marks from me for objectivity. You don't get the Harry Caray or John DeMott routine from Chick. If a Laker blows a play, he says so. If the official makes a mistake for or against the Lakers, he tells you. When I grow up, I'd like to be just like Chick.

Going against the grain made Howard Cosell the number one guy in the sports broadcast business for nearly two decades, and it's helped me prosper, too. But it is possible, albeit unusual, to be an honest and admirable sportscaster without being anti-establishment. Vin Scully, Lindsey Nelson, and Chick Hearn are all the proof you need.

CHAPTER 9

How Time Slips Away

It would have been hard for me to imagine how many opportunities I'd have over the years in San Diego. In a way what I'm doing is an extension of my college years, when I worked nearly nonstop. It was like that when I was a kid, too. From the time I was 11, I had a summer job. I worked at a laundry then for $5 a week. At 12 I was working on a truck that drove around filling cigarette machines. At 13 I was a short-order cook at a New Jersey hotel. Next I was a paper boy. It was always work, work, work. The pattern hasn't changed. Now I have the morning and afternoon radio shows. The TV sports segments at 5 and 11. Padre games on the cable and radio broadcasts on the road. Padre talk show. Charger games. I keep saying I'm going to slow down.

You might be interested in how I escape from the sports scene. Well, I'm pretty much a true San Diegan in this regard. I love to go out on the boat I bought a few years ago. No phone, nobody to recognize me. Or so I thought. The first day out on the bay, up comes a Navy cruiser steaming into the 32nd Street pier. All of a sudden I'm jolted by this great blaring bullhorn crying, "Hey, Ted! How ya doin'?" I swear, a bunch of sailors were calling to me from the deck. They must have recognized me from a distance of 300 yards. My first thought was I'd made another dumb investment. If this was privacy, I was in trouble.

But I was wrong about that. I have all the privacy I need when I can find the time to take the boat out. I love to get out on the bay with the sun in my face and nothing to think about. But I just don't have the time to get out as often as I'd like.

My boat is a 33-footer. No radar or serious stuff you would use for fishing. I hate to fish, by the way. It's the most boring sport in the world. I always get calls from people asking why I don't give the fishing catches. Heck, I'd rather *fish* than talk about it. I can certainly think of more exciting TV fare.

Anyway, my boat is named Travel Travel, after a travel agency I used to own. The boat has outlasted the travel agency. It might be nice to just sail away, but I never take anything longer than a day cruise. And even when I can't get out, I love to sit in the sun beside my pool or on the beach, read a book, and think about anything other than what I'll talk about at five and eleven o'clock. That's good times for me. I don't disco or do drugs. Just a day in the sun is all I need.

The idea of buying the boat originated in 1981 when the travel agency asked me to accompany a group on a promotional cruise in the Caribbean. I had a great time. It was like being on a floating hotel with dinner at a top restaurant every night. The gentle rocking motion of the ship made sleep an experience akin to being back in the womb. There was all the sunshine I could ever ask for, plenty of room to jog on deck, even midnight buffets, much to the detriment of my waistline. Having a boat seemed the ideal way to get away from the tensions of my job.

When I bought the boat, I knew next to nothing

about life as a mariner. I just felt my way along. I read Chapman's book on piloting and talked to a lot of old salts for advice. Now I'm able to at least sound nautical by saying something like, "Avast, let's go to starboard and see what's going on, mate."

My only regret about the boat is the meager return relative to the expense of maintenance. As I said, it's a great getaway, but the cost is astronomical. You know the definition of a boat — a giant hole in the water into which you throw money. It sits there in its slip, eroding, like a beach. It requires endless sanding, painting, and polishing. For all this maintenance, I may average a day trip once a month. Either the weather is lousy or my schedule simply won't permit me to get away. I'll tell you this: if you have to ask how much it costs, you truly can't afford it.

Part of my problem is that I don't do a very efficient job managing my time. I detest the practice of keeping one of those little lists of things to do each day. I just am not that organized. The only place I ever see a clear desk is at a furniture store. I'm trying to become more organized and efficient, because I've realized it's the ticket to more leisure time. To expedite the process, I hired a private secretary. Not long after she started, we were going through some correspondence and came across two-year-old letters. My secretary looked like she was going to faint.

When it comes to mail, I'm a total slob. I'm deluged with packages, press releases, and personal letters, all of which I open wearing asbestos gloves. In my office at the station, you could find a dead animal buried amid all the mess and it wouldn't surprise me. Maybe it's my way of thumbing my nose at work and saying it's not that important. I was a total blockhead in this regard until I realized it was keeping me from the beach.

The schedule is brutal. In baseball season it drives me to distraction. Morning radio shows at 7:15 and 8:15, afternoon radio at 4:15 and 5:15, TV segments at 5:20 and 5:40, tape the 6:30 commentary, then head to the stadium for Padre Talk, then do the cable broadcast on 41 dates. Whew! On weekends I split for a road game on Saturday morning, then return Sunday night and start the whole process again on Monday.

I'm not seeking sympathy here. I chose this schedule. Paying alimony to two former wives has something to do with it, but it goes beyond that. I'm just insecure or realistic enough to ask myself, "How long is it going to last?" I want to ride the wave while it's there. Sure, my hair is turning gray and I'm under a lot of stress, but I just can't refuse when someone offers me a bundle of money to take on another assignment.

In addition to the broadcast chores, I make three or four luncheon speeches and do four or five banquets or roasts each month. I do the booking myself, and I'm booked months in advance. I'm probably doing the work of three men, and I don't mean Larry, Curly, and Moe.

I love talking to live groups. One of my favorites was an appearance I made with Billy Shields and Ed White of the Chargers at the San Dieguito Boys Club. We were enjoying a panel discussion when a hand shot up in back and this kid says, "They told us we would have ice cream and cake when you were all done. So could you please hurry up?"

Another time I was speaking to the San Diego Glass Dealers Association at a hotel in Mission Valley. The very first question was from a lady who asked, "Excuse me, do you know where the women's restroom is?" People were hysterical. I was in shock.

These appearances generate a little extra adrenalin. It's good for the ego *and* the bottom line. Not that I rake it in like Cosell, whose speaking fee is on the order of $10,000, I believe. With that kind of fee, he probably got the idea people really liked him, when what they actually wanted was to be in his presence. On a Barbara Walters special he seemed surprised when she asked why he was so unpopular. He confused being well-known with being liked. I try not to make that mistake.

I think I know the reason Howard was crucified for years by sports writers. Jealousy. I read a newspaper article in which the salaries of sports columnists were discussed. The average was $46,700. It was reported that a couple of really top guys were getting $100,000. Wow. There are weekend sportscasters in Chicago making that. There are anchormen in New York who pay more taxes than the top sports columnists gross. It's easy to see why the columnists take shots at Cosell and us guys in the TV biz.

I know some newspaper guys who are creative and hard-working, yet they're sweating for chump change. They realize the printed word lacks power compared to Cosell or some other commentator on national television. But I think it's misguided to blame broadcasters for the fact they make more than newspaper guys. The print guys should be after their unions or their employers, who've kept them down for all these years.

There's an attitudinal problem with some print guys. A dumb attitude, if you ask me. Some columnists I read about were quoted as saying they didn't sell any newspapers with their work. My God! Don't say that! If you say it, why should your boss pay you? Instead of being jealous, these writers ought to thank broadcast people for raising the scale, for creating the awareness that a media guy can be worth $1.5 million. If Cosell or Scully or Marv Albert makes more than $1 million, eventually some newspaper guy ought to receive big bucks, too.

By the same token, broadcasters should never be jealous of others making big money, either. When Michael Tuck came to San Diego in 1978, he was making $90,000. At the time, I was getting $30,000. Tuck had already turned down one offer from KFMB — a strategy that helps get you more money. It makes them think you must be terrific. Like Groucho Marx said, he wouldn't want to belong to a country club that would have him as a member. In a sense I wouldn't want to work for a TV station that wanted me too bad.

But to get back to Mike Tuck. I was never jealous of his salary. I want to see everybody do well, and I hope I'll be included when the time comes for a raise. The principle is this: if they're used to paying $90,000, or $190,000, it seems less outrageous when the guys making less ask for a pay hike. How many times have we seen this in baseball, like most recently when Ozzie Smith got a $2 million salary from the St. Louis Cardinals. Gussie Busch had refused to pay Bruce Sutter and Keith Hernandez, and he lost them to other teams. He had to meet the going wage when Ozzie threatened to go free agent. Other players had created the $2 million standard. Ozzie took advantage of it.

When Walter Jacobson of Chicago became the first local anchorman to get a $1 million salary, I was happy. Who cares if he's worth it? Let the employer decide that. That salary threshold can only help everyone else in the business. Weather and sports guys will get more, too, it says here. How come newspaper guys can't figure that out?

Newspaper guys like to think of themselves as

working stiffs. They seem to take pride in degrading themselves. But, I must say, certain members of the press corps are hypocrites. Take Dick Young of the *New York Post*. He's one of the best-known and influential columnists of the last 30 years. He has for years been ripping Cosell as Howie the Shill. Some of my younger readers may be interested to know that Young, back in the 1950s, traveled with the Brooklyn Dodgers, at the ball club's expense. Who knows how many seedy stories he suppressed. Jim Bouton later wrote a bestseller about what happened in the hotels and clubhouses, but Dick Young never broke a single story along those lines, although he must have seen his share. The point is, it's easy to deify the jocks and then turn around and castigate a broadcaster for being a shill.

Like Cosell, Young has been selling papers for decades by being irascible. Many of his opinions date from the early eighteenth century. But when a few TV guys dared to be feisty and opinionated, Young took umbrage. People read Dick Young because he will refer to a ballplayer as a sick druggie, or some phrase like that. He calls for pushers to be exterminated. Fine. But grant broadcasters the same privilege, please.

Dick Young is never boring, and I get a kick out of reading him, but the hypocrisy extends through several layers. He criticizes athletes for their lack of loyalty in moving from one team to another, depending on who waves the biggest moneybag. Then Young proves himself equally as mercenary by jumping from the *New York Daily News* to the *New York Post*. Right on, Dick.

While I'm at it, I'll tell you what I think about some other writers.

Larry King, a very skilled radio interviewer, does an asinine column for *The Sporting News*. He seems to have patterned it after Joe Falls, another *Sporting News* regular. These guys give you a list of things they like, broken up into five-word sentences followed by three dots. For example: I never met a meatball sandwich I didn't like . . . I just love the smell of hot dogs at the ball park . . . Don't you think Rick Dempsey is a great catcher? . . . I read this crap for the laughs.

Jim Murray of the *Los Angeles Times* used to be the absolute best, but now he's lost his fast ball. He seems to have run out of ideas, and he's just repeating himself. Murray should be relegated to page 3, or page 6 and Scott Ostler belongs on page 1.

Ostler, in my opinion, is now the best columnist in the country. He is consistently funny, the Mike Royko of sports. I love his column, "The Answer Man." During the 1984 National League playoffs, he commented on the decision to use only four substitute umpires when the regular umps were on strike. The custom in the playoffs is to have six arbiters. Ostler wrote, "Well, yeah, but the pregame entertainment was terrific. They booked the Three Tops and the Kingston Duo." You have to be something special to write like that on a regular basis.

I also like Steve Harvey, who writes "The Bottom 10" for The *L. A. Times*. One of my favorite lines concerned Jim Marshall of the Minnesota Vikings, who holds the pro football record for fumbles recovered. Harvey quipped, "That record is amazing because Wendell Tyler didn't come into the league until the end of Jim's career."

Among San Diego writers, I prefer Tom Cushman and Wayne Lockwood to Barry Lorge. I've had a running battle with Lorge, and I regret the fact, because I think he's a nice, learned man. He's probably forgotten more sports than I know. I certainly wasn't insulted when he was named the successor to Jack Murphy, a guy I always believed was in the Chargers' pocket. I was never entertained by Murphy's columns on hunting and fishing. He was just too establishment for my taste. When Murphy died, I thought the job should have gone to Wayne Lockwood, who is a stronger writer than Lorge. But the *Union* editors seemed to feel it was desirable to hire a guy who had worked for the prestigious *Washington Post*. Lorge was a terrific tennis writer at the *Post*, but here he seems to have trouble realizing there's more to life than tennis. He hasn't really shown a feel for the streets or the ability to write with feeling about sports other than tennis. Still, I tend to agree with another *Union* writer, Phil Collier, who said my feud with Lorge is beneath both of us. I started it, I'll admit it. I can't seem to keep my big mouth shut.

This may surprise some readers, but I think I am mellowing. I don't want to be a constant criticizer.

CHAPTER 10

Numbers Are
a Guy's Best Friend

Life's full of little indignities. We in broadcasting
are not exempt. We are widely recognized and well paid,
but we are also subject to certain curses known to no
other group of workers. Foremost is a little item known
as the galvanic skin response test. You've probably never
heard of it if you've never clipped a microphone to your
lapel on a daily basis. It's one of the lesser-known
measuring sticks of a broadcaster's popularity and effec-
tiveness as a communicator. It's also pretty damn close
to a violation of human rights, in my opinion.

The idea behind the galvanic skin response test is to
determine who's macho and who's not. As a rather
crude add-on to the Nielsen and Arbitron ratings, the
galvanic test is designed to help the marketing people
determine a male broadcaster's ability to reach a certain
group — women, aged 18–49, who happen to constitute
the major advertising target group. These marketing
whizzes conduct their test by hiring a panel of women,
renting a hotel room equipped with TV, and wiring the
women to machines that measure the level of skin
moisture on the palms of the hands as an indication of
sexual arousal as they watch the news, weather, and

sports personnel. It's a simple test. If a woman is turned on by the anchorman, she gets wet, and the anchor is a hit with the galvanic skin response testers. Now athletes have been known to complain about undergoing urinalysis for drug screening, but they never have to put up with anything as degrading as the galvanic test.

The anchorman on a St. Louis station was going to be fired once because he did poorly on the wetness test. But the station had to relent when the St. Louis newspapers got hold of the story, suggesting that someone at the station was daft. The public reaction was enormous, in the vein of, "I don't care if he turns me on, just give me the news. Let somebody else make me wet."

I won't soon forget the time when Mike Tuck and I were in Philadelphia and he turned to me during a commercial and said, "You better do good today. They're at the Holiday Inn across the street doing the galvanic skin response test." That was the first time I ever heard of it. It seemed grossly unfair, and still does. I wonder what test they'd use in San Francisco? Tuck and I made a pact that if either of us ever got fired because we didn't make the women wet enough, we would never tell. We'd make up something — like it was terminal herpes, or rape. Anything but failure to make the women wet.

Athletes routinely justify their salaries by saying their careers can be ended at any moment by injury. I guess the same sort of thing applies to the TV biz, with the threat of being fired because of poor ratings. Admittedly, the galvanic skin test is an aberration, but the Nielsens and Arbitrons are very much with us, a fact of life no broadcaster can overlook.

In case you haven't heard, the Nielsens and Arbitrons are surveys conducted to determine who is watching TV. The findings are broken down by age group, income, locale, and other factors. The Nielsen ratings are obtained from a little black box hooked up to the TV sets of a random group of Americans. The Arbitron information is gathered from diaries sent to a random group in November, February, May, and July. Each family is requested to jot down information on which programs they watch for a period of one month.

The point of all this measuring is to be able to give advertisers very specific demographic information. Let's say a network is trying to line up advertisers for a golf tournament. They can go to a sponsor — say, Cadillac — and produce last year's data, which might show that the average income of families tuning in to this tournament was $75,000. Hence, this tournament would be an ideal vehicle to reach this target group of high-income families. With a bowling tournament, beer and tires might be the obvious sponsors because of a predominantly blue-collar audience.

The Nielsen and Arbitron ratings are national in scope. But individual stations do their own studies, as well. There's a scary test in which a sample audience is shown a picture of a local TV guy. Questions are posed, such as, "Like him? Dislike him? What do you like? What do you dislike? Do you like the weather guy? The sports guy? Which stories do you like? Why?" The findings supplement the ratings, enabling stations to rank the respective popularity of their people. Thus, it's not just whether people are watching, it's also whether they care about you as a personality.

You must understand the value of one measly little rating point. In San Diego a single point is worth about $250,000 in annual advertising revenue. Thus, if a station can increase its rating from 8 to 9, it stands to make an additional quarter of a million dollars a year.

That's why stations pay so much attention to the ratings. The cost of marketing research and ratings is a small price for a station to pay to gain an edge.

Back in 1978, when Mike Tuck, Allison Ross, Clark Anthony and I started at KFMB, we were a solid number three in this market. That's the third of three, as in dead last. We very quickly went to a solid, dominant number one, a position we've occupied almost without interruption for the past seven years. The only rating period we lost was in February, 1980, during the Winter Olympics on ABC. I know I generate some negative reaction among viewers, but it's obvious I haven't chased away too many. The station wouldn't be number one if I had.

The research worked for me in Hartford, where people liked my smile, but it hurt me in Philadelphia when they decided I smiled too much. They never told me if I made enough women wet. To be fair, I may have brought trouble on myself. One story that caused me problems was a feature on the 76ers' Darryl Dawkins, who had nicknames for his dunks and called one of them the Gorilla Slam. I showed a clip from a King Kong movie along with a Dawkins dunk, which got the station a phone call from the NAACP accusing me of racism. Another time, after Evel Knievel beat up a TV executive with a baseball bat, I made the comment, "Wow, I didn't realize it was a felony to go after TV execs with a bat, and I don't see why it should be. At the most, make it a misdemeanor." Thinking back, I can see how that might have caused me some problems, in ratings and otherwise.

When the decision was made to fire me, the guy told me "You give the audience the bends." Like a deep-sea diver who ascends too fast. The guy also told me they were willing to let me out of my contract. That is, they were giving me the chance to leap before I was pushed.

I believe there are some serious Philadelphia-types in the San Diego audience, but fortunately they're not a majority. We have our serious, frustrated jocks, the Ombac group who want to kill when they play Over the Line. And they hate my guts. But these folks are outnumbered by the people who would simply rather go to the beach and have a good time than live and die with a sports team. These folks have saved me and made me employable in the market. As I've already said, I would rather go to the beach myself than to the ball park.

For the most part, research has actually helped me (and a lot of other guys), because it convinces the station we're money makers. When research shows, for instance, that Warner Wolf in New York is worth at least one rating point, his $500,000 salary can be justified by his station as an investment instead of an expenditure. It's akin to Donald Trump's decision to sign Doug Flutie, or George Steinbrenner signing Reggie Jackson. We're talking about an investment, both in advertising potential and also in publicity. There's a lot of promotional value in a big marquee name. Julius Erving in Philadelphia returns his salary, and a lot more. Dan Rather doesn't get $2 million from CBS because he's a warm personality and they like his ties. It's because he makes a difference in the ratings — a $2 million difference. Pick some other names — David Hartmann, Brent Musburger. The money is there because they build the audience, and the advertisers love a big audience. That's all there is to it.

I certainly care about the findings of these tests, but I've never tried to adjust my act accordingly. I do it my way and enjoy it. I've been lucky in San Diego. According to the research, people by and large think I'm funny. I've been told that in some markets, research shows the water pressure drops during the weather and sports segments. You follow me? That means a lot of toilets are flushing during those segments because people are bored and taking a break. That's bad news for the sports and weather guys. Talk about going down the tubes.

I've made a point of saying I don't think sports is serious, but how about the weather. I mean, who gives a damn if the temperature in Little Rock today was 89 degrees? I don't think many people care about or understand all the stuff about highs and lows and Canadian fronts. Just say if it's going to be hot or cold, or if it's going to rain.

I'll admit I've seen a few really entertaining weather guys. The best was the late Jim O'Brien in Philadelphia. He was nuts, and I mean that in a positive way. Instead of maps full of highs and lows, he would label them good guys and bad guys. A picture of a cloud with a smile might be next to a frowning thunderstorm. People loved him. The terrible thing was that he died in a sky diving accident in 1983. The station received something like 30,000 letters of condolence. People even mailed copies of the papers to Tuck and me, because they remembered we used to work alongside O'Brien.

The point I'm making here is that you have to make your stuff interesting, be it sports or weather. All too many guys in this business just recite the dull facts without making it interesting. The consequences of doing it that way can be fatal. When I worked in Oklahoma City, the station conducted a survey which ascertained that the main sportscaster, who had been on the air for ten years, was virtually unknown to the viewing audience. He was a boring guy, nobody responded to him very strongly, and when the testers showed photos of him, nobody in the testing sample even recognized him. He had the temerity to go on the air and tell the audience why he was being canned. I thought that was in questionable taste, but the story demonstrates the compelling need to reflect a little of your personality in your work.

I really believe people watch their favorites, regardless of whether or not a guy has a reputation in the industry for being outstanding. And if you can build the numbers, you can expect to be justly compensated. This is particularly true in the Los Angeles market, where a half point difference in the ratings can make more than $500,000 difference in revenue. I'm told, for example, that Stu Nahan makes $300,000 a year, and he's about as exciting as watching paint dry. He reveals no personality, but just about everyone in L. A. seems to know him, so he has a lot of value to his station. I do give him credit for that. Along the same lines, I thought Bryan Gumble, when he worked at Channel 4 in L. A., was far too serious, but people seemed to think he was wonderful, and of course he wound up as the host of NBC's Today Show. It's a fascinating subject, and one that neither I nor anyone else really understands.

Consider a radio guy, Rick Dees. He has the largest audience of anyone in the nation on morning radio, which means his station can command very high rates for advertising. He's got it all going for him. But when I listen, it doesn't sound all that funny to me. My 11-year-old laughs, so maybe that's something. Dees is turning out record albums, he's on network TV, and, I understand, he's got a movie deal. He's hot, no question.

Dees's success is easier for me to understand than

the popularity of radio talk show hosts who insult their audience by yelling and screaming and hanging up on callers. Millions tune in to hear these guys rant and rave, so the talk show hosts make a fortune. That's what the ratings will do for you. Just build up the numbers. They're money in the bank.

When the ratings indicate that a guy is popular, his station is stuck with him, for better or worse. Take Jerry Dunphy, a star in Los Angeles. I read a parody of his style, referring to it as Eyewitless News. He's one of those guys who's more concerned with hair, makeup, and the sound of his voice, just like the Ted Knight character on the old *Mary Tyler Moore Show*.

The ratings pump up the ego, too. I'm thinking of how Tom Brokaw's agent once telephoned NBC and complained that the lettering behind Brokaw's head was too big and it was detracting from Tom's appearance. NBC caved in and made it the *Nightly News with Tom Brokaw*, and the anchorman's head got the prominence it deserves.

The superficiality of some anchors astounds me. An anchorperson is supposed to be educated and worldly, correct? Well, when Pablo Picasso died, an anchorperson of my acquaintance went to the producer and asked, "Who is this Pablo Pick-a-so?" Another anchor I know once described an emergency landing at "Dules" International Airport in Washington. When Lady Di got married, there was an anchor who said her husband was the Prince of Whales, as in Shamu. My favorite is probably the story about an astute political reporter named Martin Agronsky. When teleprompters were first introduced, Agronsky was a bit uncomfortable with the technology, and he tended to read everything without looking up. His show always closed with the same phrase, but on April Fools' Day, his script writer played a trick. As he bade goodnight to his audience, Agronsky said, "That's the news. From all of us here at WTOP, good evening, I'm Peter Rabbit."

CHAPTER 11

In the Land of Human Beings

I don't know how long it will last. I try not to think about it too much. While the ratings are there, I'm going to enjoy it, ride this wave as far as it takes me. When the ratings are good, management stays off my back, and that's a nice situation for anybody. I don't run into a lot of interference.

I'll tell you a sure sign that I'm in trouble in the ratings war. When you see me popping out doing three or four commercials for automobile dealers, or whomever, you'll know. I don't do any of that stuff right now because I don't need it. But if you see me plugging local products, you'll know I'm coming to the end of the line.

As for being number one, I don't get a big thrill from being on top. It's nice, but I'm not an overtly competitive, cutthroat person. In other markets, I've been friendly with rivals at other stations. We had good clean competition, and when work was done, we could get together for dinner or a few drinks, and nobody's ego would intrude. There was never any badmouthing in public, or in private, so far as I knew.

Man, but it's different here. Easterners talk about San Diego being laid back and having low-key media.

Maybe so, but I've never seen a town where there was so much jealousy among the various members of the media. Arrogant snobs like Paul Bloom and Harold Green — who have graced the airwaves on rival stations — start my competitive juices flowing. Green, who has been known to sling typewriters at people in his own newsroom, once wrote a condescending letter to Mike Tuck. This was after Green had moved to Los Angeles and had won some award, which he was going to receive at a banquet. "Dear Mike," he wrote, "it would be nice if you could join us. I'm sure this is as close as you're ever going to get to the L. A. market." That's how petty Green is.

There's been a lot of pettiness and jealousy here that I never anticipated on the basis of my work in other cities. Among others, Mike Smith has taken numerous shots at me in the press. The effect is to make me care about the ratings and really want to win.

One of the crummier episodes of petty competition took place during the 1984 National League playoffs. I had purchased some tickets — at face value — from the Padres. I gave some to friends and sold others — at face value — to a few colleagues. I was doing them a favor, because the tickets were otherwise unavailable. I was about to do my 5:20 sports segment live from the stadium parking lot when I realized I had four tickets in my pocket and would be out $100 if I didn't somehow dispose of them. As fate would have it, a woman from Nebraska saw me and started a conversation, chiding me about always picking on the Cornhuskers' football team. Then she asked me if I happened to have any extra tickets for the game, which, of course, I did. I told her I would sell them to her at face value.

At that moment, we were approached by a security

man, who obviously thought I was going to scalp the tickets. He told me it was against the law to sell anything on city property without a license. I admitted I did not know of that statute and also said that while ignorance is no excuse, I was in no case trying to scalp the tickets. He said, fine, but don't do it again. And I thought that was the end of it.

A half hour later, I was up in the press box having a bite of supper when a friend sat down and said Kathy Clark of Channel 39 had reported I was scalping tickets. My initial reaction was, "Now isn't that typical of the smalltimers in this town. Nail your colleagues, try to drag 'em down, and don't bother to check the facts." There was a reference to the matter the next morning in Tom Blair's column in the *San Diego Union*. Blair and Neil Morgan of *The Tribune* are like the *People* magazine of San Diego journalism. Blair also implied I was trying to scalp the tickets, and he never bothered to check with me, either.

Perhaps that story will give you a feel for what I mean when I refer to the pettiness of the market. I've made a conscious effort over the years to overcome my innate tendencies to burn and rage and be competitive, and by and large I've succeeded. But sometimes I can feel the old urge burning inside me again. At those moments it's almost like I never left New York.

Where I grew up it seemed like everybody had a little pilot light in their stomach. It was always, "Get outta my way, I was in line first." Naturally, I developed that sort of approach. My parents and forebears were like that, so it may be a matter of genetics as well as environment. I was destined to be a driven, compulsive person, and there was little I could do about it until I grew up and left New York.

My Dad, in particular, had a major-league pilot light. He was a coiled top. People think I'm a type A personality — a heart attack waiting to happen, but I'm nothing compared to my father. And I've tried to change. So far as I could tell, my Dad never really changed. He died at age 64 of a heart attack. A lot of what I am — in terms of getting angry about injustice and hypocrisy in sports — comes from my New York background.

Back then, there was a constant intense pressure to hustle for a job and make a little extra money. The first day of summer vacation after eighth grade, my Dad looked at me and said, "Got a job yet?" That has stuck with me all my life. The work ethic has never left me. I say I'm going to modify it, but I haven't really cut back. I do try to relax when I'm not working. I don't want to be like so many compulsive people who curse and scream when they don't make it through a green light. I don't need the high blood pressure and clogged arteries that result from such an approach to life. Sports is only a game, and this is your only life, so why not loosen up and enjoy it? I really want to overcome my tendencies in the other direction.

My Dad was a warrior. A real warrior. Save your money. Be first in line. Don't trust anybody. His own father raised him in that mold, and so he raised me the only way he had ever known.

It's sad, because I really don't know much about my father's background. We never talked about it. When I watch a TV sitcom and see family members having a conversation, it seems unreal to me. My family life was never like *Ozzie and Harriet* or *Father Knows Best*. As a child I had no way to know that a father could talk to his son in ways other than, "Take that garbage out!" I don't remember my Dad ever using a normal conversational tone with his children. There was no conversation at the dinner table, because Dad was always trying to hear the news on the radio. A friend of mine confided that his father knew several languages and encouraged his kids to converse in different tongues at dinner. That seemed neat. We never conversed in English, much less French.

I believe my father's parents emigrated to New York from Germany, and I think my mother's family was from Austria. But I don't know why they came to this country, or what they did for a living. I don't remember my grandparents, who died when I was quite young. I regret all this ignorance about my roots and my ancestry.

I suspect my father grew up in more trying circumstances than I did, and I don't want to sound too bitter. I believe it's possible to change and overcome your tendencies. In Wayne Dyer's book *The Erroneous Zones* the point is made that using your parents as an excuse is a cop-out. I want to slow down, stop bitching, and have a good time. It just isn't worth having a heart attack and pushing up daisies.

I have no idea what made my Dad happy, what turned him on, or what he enjoyed. He liked to read the papers and listen to the radio. He worked as a wine salesman, making calls on distributorships in the Bronx. It's hard to imagine that he was a good salesman, because he didn't like people. He was in a bad mood that lasted 64 years. Driving around the Bronx in his stripped-down car, with no radio or air conditioning, couldn't have been much fun for him. It's conceivable to me that he was dissatisfied with his marriage, and he may have regretted having children. That's speculation, he never said anything about it to me. I really don't know what he thought about anything. He never talked about his own childhood, and I couldn't even tell you what neighborhood in Brooklyn he lived in. He had five or six brothers and sisters, but we never socialized with any of them. One of his sisters moved to California and became a human being, but she didn't know Dad well enough to give me any insight. It would be nice if I could somehow talk to him and get answers to some of these things.

I do know this much: Dad would be right at home in the New York City of 1985. If anything, it's a more intense place than it was when I was growing up. Probably the biggest thing that ever happened to me was getting away and meeting some real people. After 18 years there, I had no conception of what it was like to be friendly to anyone in public. The waitress barks, "Whaddya want?" Joe Bauer has a line about being in New York and approaching this hooker and she screams, "Whaddya want?"

Imagine the culture shock I experienced in leaving New York as an uptight 18-year-old college freshman enrolling at Oklahoma State University in Stillwater, Oklahoma. Walk down the street and people say, "Howdy!" just like Roy Rogers and Dale Evans. I wasn't sure I was still in the continental United States, but I didn't recall anyone checking my passport. Anyway, the first day I was there I went into a five-and-dime store to buy some school supplies. As I was checking out, the checker, a cute young girl, looked at me and said sweetly, "How ya doin?" She might as well have blasted me with a stun gun. Then she bagged my stuff and gave me my change. "Come back," she added. That really got me. Being new to the territory, I didn't know she simply

meant to drop into the store again if I needed more supplies. What I did was to stop in my tracks, do an about-
face and walk back to the cash register. I thought I had
forgotten my change. That was an awkward moment,
but not really so terrible. I was in the land of human beings for the first time in my life.

CHAPTER 12

As Long As I Got Some Bread

Among the elements missing from my childhood was a briefing on Jewish tradition. My Dad never taught me a thing about what it was to be a Jew. I don't consider myself religious, and I strongly dislike theological labels of any kind. It's always seemed to me a person's faith is his own business. I don't want to know what you are. I'll fight to the death for your right to believe as you wish, but don't hate me because I have a different set of beliefs.

I am not afraid of going to hell. Jews don't believe in hell, which is convenient in my case. Religion has had very little influence on my life, but I've always been glad I was in a faith that didn't lay a lot of fire and brimstone on you. I pitied the Catholic kids with their burden of guilt. It seemed like a means of control.

I was not unaware of anti-Semitism in my youth. In the third grade the kids I hung around with during lunch were Italian kids mostly. One day we were talking about Mr. Gallagher, the eighth grade science teacher. He was in charge of discipline in the lunch room, a tough guy, and students feared him. We were throwing food or doing something else likely to get us in trouble, when one of my buddies said, "That Gallagher, he's such a Jew." That was a pretty traumatic moment for me. It was like a black kid hearing the word "nigger" for the first time. That comment blew me away.

There were some parts of Passover I hated — such as the prohibition on eating bread for ten days. I can't keep it a secret any longer. I snuck all the time. I'd go down to the corner deli, called Andy's Delicadandy, and eat sandwiches while my mother was away or not paying attention. That was my first great sin in life. Would God send anybody to hell for eating bread? In my household, the answer seemed to be "yes," because all the bread had to be out of the house before Passover began. I never lasted more than the first two days without sneaking.

As an adult, I've always had a weight problem, and a large part of it originated with the New York food I powered down as a kid. To a New York Jew, eating is a sport, like football, baseball, or basketball. I practically lived at Andy's, where I would order sandwiches, chips, and cupcakes. There was also a deli up the street from Roosevelt High in Yonkers. And there was a Nathan's, where we would go for hot dogs and sandwiches. Everything in Nathan's smelled deep fried, even the waiters. The food was greasy, and I loved it. Food was unquestionably a big part of my life. I'd come home from school, eat a snack and look forward to another after supper. I have finally learned I can't eat so compulsively, or I'll gain excessive amounts of weight and be unhappy with myself. It wasn't easy to learn moderation.

For that matter, it wasn't easy for anyone in our family to eat in moderation. My dad had a mighty gut, and my brother has had to battle obesity. We had the typical Jewish mom, whose first commandment was, "EAT! Eat three plates. It makes me feel good when you eat." I'm not sure about the origin of that tradition — perhaps it goes back to the starvation the Jews knew in Europe — but it's sure made my life tougher. As doctors have since discovered, the fat cells you develop as a kid never go away. It takes a lot of jogging to defeat those fat cells.

I guess it helped to have my pilot light set on high, to metabolize all the heavy food we consumed in the Leitner apartment. The comedian Buddy Hackett grew up in New York and assumed it was normal to have heartburn. He had it for 20 years and didn't know any better until he joined the Army. He was used to eating that greasy, heavy stuff served by Jewish mothers, and he thought it was perfectly natural to walk around with a scowl going, "Bllleeeech!" My Dad was like that, forever belching. We ate Americanized food, nothing kosher. Potato pancakes, meat, bread. I never had a salad until I went to college. We were about as Jewish as Methodists. We never had barbecue or a charcoal grill. There was no place to put a grill unless you wanted to burn down the apartment next door.

While I was a kid, my metabolism was such that I could eat all day and not gain an ounce. You could put a horse between two slices of bread, and I'd eat it and stay slim. If you could make a sandwich out of it, I'd eat it. The bread didn't matter — rye, wheat, bagels. If it's on a sandwich, I will consume it, and that's still my favorite kind of eating.

As I've indicated, my mother's consuming passion was food, shopping for it, cooking it, and seeing it eaten. She couldn't pass a bakery without buying a cake. She was forever bringing home cold cuts and candy. She knew how much food excited us, and she had never heard of cholesterol.

To this day I associate food with places. If I'm back east with the Padres, I might call some friends and visit the Jersey shore. And inevitably I'm assaulted by the smell of hotdogs and pizza and cotton candy and popcorn, all the smells of the boardwalk. Many foods are prepared differently in California, but once I had pizza slices at the Sports Arena, and the sauce was the same I remembered from the Jersey shore as a kid. Waves of nostalgia came over me, and I was transported back to my boyhood: school over, time for baseball, a visit to the shore. For me, foods trigger that kind of response all the time.

My mother had a tendency to be overly sentimental, and that's a trait I share with her. One year, after my brother and I went to college, we were home for Christmas. We were sitting at the table with Mom, looking through an old yearbook, and she started to cry as she read some of those saccharine inscriptions that go into yearbooks. I have the same tendency. In fact, I keep my yearbook right by my desk in my office at home. I thumb through it, and the past returns, like it never left.

When summer comes, I have to fight the sadness as I lie in my bed on a warm Saturday morning and listen to the kids playing outside. I think back to family times together on the Jersey shore. There were no pressures, no deadlines, no alimony, no nothing. When those waves of nostalgia hit me, I can get quite depressed. I try not to look back too often. George Burns, in his autobiography, described the pain of missing Gracie Allen and how wiped out he was. Then he said something profound: "It's great to have a past, but you can't live in it." I realize I can't think about my mother all the time, or bring her back from the grave. Although it seems like it was so much better when I was with her, it probably wouldn't be the same if somehow I could go back.

My nostalgia really is focused on my mother. The thing about the past is that she was there. When I was away at school for the first time, and later when I was getting into broadcasting, I didn't have much trouble coping with the long separations, because she was still alive. I didn't go home often, but she was still there, and I could call if I needed to talk. I took her for granted. She was there, and now she isn't there. It's a struggle to make it fun when I think about pizza and hotdogs at the Jersey shore, because none of it is recapturable. As I get older, and presumably smarter, I have to fight off the remembrances.

The positive side of this is that at least she was there when I was growing up and didn't die when I was 12. I have no conception of which way I would have gone if that had happened. I was so lucky she lived through my childhood and into my thirties. I try to reinforce that concept, but it's not easy, because I miss her so much.

I wish I'd visited her more often when I was a young adult. I didn't do it the way it should have been done. I have a lot of regrets, and there is utterly nothing I can do about it. Now I want to make sure I don't look back in another ten years and say, "You fool, you had it all, your kids were young and you didn't enjoy it." If you make the same mistakes twice, you're *really* a fool.

My parents were such absolute opposites, it's difficult to fathom the bond. One was a miserable, evil-tempered man, the other was a woman for whom kids were the world and who had a smile for everybody. Both of them are inside me, and my task is to keep him in and let her out. Bizarre.

I respect and envy people with a strong belief in the hereafter. The belief you will see your parents and friends again is a lovely thought, but I don't have that belief. When your mother is gone, you've lost a person who loved you unconditionally, as no one else ever will, and that is the greatest loss you can endure.

When I was three or four years old, I'd accompany Mom on shopping trips. We took the trolley or a rickety old bus. One day I went to the bathroom in my pants — just couldn't hold it — as we were returning home. I'd never messed up my pants since I'd been potty trained, and I was worried about what her reaction was going to be. I felt *very* sheepish, but her reaction was, "No big deal. We'll just change it." It was like having the weight of the world lifted from my shoulders. I try to put that sort of patience and understanding into handling my own kids, but sometimes I have the immediate father reaction, "Goddamit, I'm busy, son!" Then I'll say to myself, "Hey, wait! Remember! Don't be a schmuck!" I do my best to react in a positive manner.

During the summers, my mother would go to her job in Manhattan for the first three days of the week and then, each Wednesday night, she would take the train from Grand Central to the Jersey shore. Since my Dad would stay in the Bronx until Friday night, we had two days of uninterrupted peace and tranquillity. My brother Lou and I would go to the train station in Bradley Beach to meet my mother when she arrived. It seemed as if she would always disembark on the opposite side of the platform from us, and I can remember looking under the train for the sight of her feet descending the steps. I was always afraid she had missed the train — until I saw her heels and skirt, which I recognized instantly. Then the train would pull out, and she'd be standing there, smiling, and we'd walk off toward the boarding house, stopping along the way for something to eat, of course. A friend once remarked that Mom was in all her glory when Dad wasn't there, and I could see it.

One of the more embarrassing incidents of my childhood happened when Mom and Dad got into a fight. My Mom had loaned some money to a friend and Dad was after her to collect it. In fact, he had gone to her friend and tried to collect himself. It was on a Sunday night, and I had walked both of them back to the car for their trip back to Manhattan. They were arguing the whole way. Certain the neighbors had heard all of it, I went around the back of the boarding house and crawled through the bushes so I wouldn't have to face any of them.

My memories of the fighting go back to the time I was five or six, and I'm sure it was going on even earlier. It was such a stupid way to live. I was always terribly uncomfortable when my parents got into it, with all the cursing and tears.

When I was older I interceded during their fights. I'd grab Dad and drag him away. I hated that stuff. It made me sad and influenced my life drastically — I've left two marriages that I thought might turn out the same way. It may have been a knee-jerk reaction on my part, but I simply would not treat a woman the way my mother was treated. I wouldn't have my children watching me talk to a woman with disrespect and anger and foul language. And I didn't know any other way to handle the situation.

The biggest fear in my life has been that I would wind up like my Dad. That fear led me to part with thousands of dollars in divorce settlements and alimony because I refused to wind up in an unhappy marriage full of screaming and abuse and maybe cheating on the side. I've put up with a lot and been jacked around by attorneys because of my unwillingness to endure what my parents went through. Better that I should see my children once or twice a week, and we should all enjoy it, than subject them to the sort of childhood I experienced.

Since I never learned how to converse with an adult, it was difficult for me to tell my mother how much she meant to me. Later, when she was sick, I put my feelings into a long letter and mailed it to her nursing home in New York. I wanted her to understand how much I appreciated what she had done. Every morning she would leave home at 5 a.m. for her commute to the garment district in Manhattan. She would have to take a cab, a bus, and the subway to get there, and then reverse the process in the afternoon, fix us dinner, and stay up until ten or eleven at night helping with homework or doing crosswords. For 18 years that was her routine, and it was a great sacrifice. In my letter I spelled out my feelings. Unbeknownst to my father, she had maintained a secret savings account, and during my college years, she would regularly send me a letter with three $10 bills in it. I put all my gratitude into the letter I sent her at the nursing home, how she made me feel loved like nobody's business. I couldn't have made it without her constant affection. When I think of children in homes with *two* abusive parents, it makes me want to scream.

CHAPTER 13

To Get Along, Be Grumpy

One of the greatest compliments ever paid me came from Ray Kroc. On the occasion of his eightieth birthday (which the Padres celebrated with a big night at the stadium), Ray requested that two videotapes be shown in his private box. One of the tapes was of Ronald Reagan, at Ray's request. The other was of me. Frankly, I was astounded. This isn't my ego bursting out, it's just a statement of the surprise I felt when Padre employees told me I was one of Ray's favorites.

Understand, I had never been soft on Ray. Many times I criticized him for hiring the wrong people and making dumb trades or wasting millions on players like Gene Tenace and Oscar Gamble. Ray was a lovable guy, but if he had run McDonald's the way he ran the Padres, nobody would know what a Big Mac was. I said that on the air, but he wasn't offended, and I'm told he thought I was a funny guy. I was just as critical of Ray as I was of Gene Klein, but their reactions to the criticism illustrate the differences in the two men. Gene is all businessman, with icewater running through his veins. Ray had a sense of humor and a sense of family that I think eventually was conveyed to his ball club. It probably had a lot to do with helping the Padres win the National League pennant in 1984.

Ray and I got along for the same reason that I have a fairly compatible relationship with Dick Williams. Dick has a lot of grumpiness and moodiness in him, and I can identify with those qualities. Dick's an old-fashioned guy and so am I. He has guts, and maybe he can relate to me on that score. He knows I don't give a damn if a ballplayer doesn't like me, and that's certainly true of him as well. If I was a namby-pamby, like some of the guys in the media, Dick would run me into the ground. For the most part I have gotten along well with Dick.

I was once told by Peter Gammons of the *Boston Globe* that he had been in Dick's office after a game along with several players who were bitching about something I'd said. According to Gammons' report, Dick was defending me. "At least he's funny and entertaining," Dick said. He recognized I was no viper. I assume he has a good opinion of me. The essential thing about Dick Williams is this: he gets results. Many players hate him. That's no secret. But to knock him is a waste of time. I certainly don't believe Dick is above criticism, but he hates it just the same.

Dick just doesn't realize that criticism, in the form of second-guessing by the fans and media, is as inevitably a part of the baseball mix as hotdogs and beer. Baseball, for God's sake, is arguing whether the manager should have pinch-hit sooner, or gone with the left-handed reliever, or bunted the guy over in the third inning. Dick takes personal umbrage at all that. How dare anyone second-guess him! Dick must be thinking, "Hey, I've been managing for 20 years and won all these pennants and World Series, how can some dumb writer or broadcaster second-guess me?" This attitude extends to the executive suite, as well, and in part, it cost him his job in Montreal, where he managed before coming to San Diego. Anytime John McHale, the Expos president, made a suggestion, Dick took it as a form of second-guessing. I've got nothing against Dick, but I have to say second-guessing the manager is as American as Babe Ruth.

Dick's battle with Barry Bloom of the *San Diego Tribune* is indicative of how sensitive he is. Barry had a running battle with Dick all through the 1984 season, and at one point the manager barred the writer from his office. I suspect there's been a Bloom in every city where Dick has managed — a writer who dared criticize and jump on his case. I don't know if Dick likes or even respects Bloom, but I have to believe he'd concede that Barry has guts. Barry, in fact, has more guts than I do. I have my little ivory tower that protects me from having to be in the everyday line of fire in the locker room. Barry has to go in there every day and get his quotes, just like all the regular beat writers. It's not a very pleasant experience when you're around the same group of 25 players for seven months.

Dick has always been cordial with me, which leads me to think he may not hear everything I say about him. I recall an instance during the '84 season when Dick climbed on Tony Gwynn. Tony was leading the league in hitting, and serving as a model for everyone on the team with his hustle on defense and on the bases. One day it happened that Tony dropped a fly ball in Candlestick Park, which has some of the toughest conditions in baseball. On a sunny, windy day, I dare say Candlestick is *the* toughest place for an outfielder in all of American baseball. Gwynn made a relatively harmless error in a game the Padres went on to win, but Williams was critical of him in his postgame press conference. "That ball has got to be caught," Dick said coldly. That seemed needlessly harsh to me, and I really nailed Dick in my commentary. "Hey, Gwynn's a kid who's playing his butt off, why not back him up," I said. It wasn't the seventh game of the World Series, and it certainly wasn't a case of a malcontent who missed a ball because he'd been goofing off and not shagging flies in the pregame workouts.

As I said, I can relate to Dick's grumpy personality, but not when it's reduced to nitpicking. In many cases, it's actually counterproductive and doesn't bring out the best in the ballplayers. Still, I have to insist that it's dumb of me or anyone to complain too much about Dick, because he's produced in Boston, Oakland, and San Diego.

I am in no way giving Williams all the credit for the Padres' transformation. Back in 1980, Ballard Smith, the team president, made a brilliant move in making Jack McKeon general manager. Jack's trades probably have as much or more to do with building a pennant winner as anything. Without the trades that brought the Padres Garry Templeton, Terry Kennedy, Alan Wiggins, Carmelo Martinez, and many others, there's no way the team would have progressed as fast as it did. Likewise, if Joan Kroc hadn't been willing to invest enormous sums in the likes of Steve Garvey, Rich Gossage, and Graig Nettles, it's likely the team would have remained a middle-echelon club. So there's a mix, and Dick Williams doesn't get all the credit. He's a baseball man with a huge ego, like Gene Mauch and Whitey Herzog, guys who think they know more baseball than anybody else who ever lived. I just wish Dick wasn't so threatened by every little innocent comment.

There was one incident involving Dick in 1984 that

I consider absolutely deplorable. Of course, I'm referring to his run-in with Carmelo Martinez in a Houston hotel bar. Dick had been drinking when he started picking on his leftfielder. I wasn't there, but other players were, and they filled me in on what happened. In essence, Dick picked a fight with young Martinez. Dick accused Martinez of being soft and not hitting the way he should. A motivational talk in a moment of sobriety might have been appropriate, but a bar isn't the place to get on a rookie outfielder. It's tough enough on a player when there are 30,000 critics in the stands. For a player to think the manager doesn't have confidence in him makes the job even more difficult. I know damn well Ballard Smith spoke to Dick about it and told him it shouldn't happen again. The implication was that Dick's job was at stake.

There's a rather humorous footnote to the Martinez incident, though. Dick apologized to the players that fall for his conduct with Carmelo, after the players had voted on shares of the playoff and World Series money. "It's OK, Dick, you don't have to say you're sorry," Graig Nettles called out from the back of the room. "We already voted you a full share."

I just don't think there's any excuse for screaming and cursing at human beings the way Williams does. He's from the same mold as Vince Lombardi. The idea is to get the player mad so he'll go out there and show his coach or manager. Maybe it makes a player play harder, but there has to be a better way.

There's a century-old tradition in baseball of retaliating when a player is hit by a pitch. An eye for an eye, a tooth for a tooth. Somebody is going to die if this doesn't stop. One of the classic examples of this retaliatory psychology occured in August 1984, when the

Padres played the Braves in Atlanta. Dick Williams received an unfair share of the blame for this nasty blot on the '84 season. It wasn't so much Dick's fault as it was the fault of baseball in general for condoning and perpetuating the tradition of throwing at the other side when one of your players is hit. Dick got too much blame, and Braves pitcher Pascual Perez, who started it all, got his share, too. The thing might have ended early in the game if the Padres' Ed Whitson had been able to hit Perez (as ordered), when he came to bat. Instead, the game got totally out of hand, and it was lucky no one was seriously injured in the ensuing beanbrawls.

There is no question that some player is going to die after taking a 95-mile-per-hour fastball in the face. There has been only one death recorded in the history of the big leagues, and that was back in the 1920s, but it's bound to happen again if attitudes don't change. The career of Boston's Tony Conigliaro was prematurely ended when he was hit in 1967, and the career of Houston's Dickie Thon was threatened when he was struck in 1984.

Heed my words: we're going to see a fractured skull or a cerebral hemorrhage, and then baseball will finally say, "Enough. That's it. No more. If you even think of throwing in the area of the head, you're out of the game, suspended for your next start and fined $5,000." But, unfortunately, we won't see sanctions this tough until there's blood on home plate.

I thought Barry Bloom was totally off base for laying the blame for the beanbrawl on Dick Williams. He said Williams was a bully and the players were simply following orders. There was more to it than that, as I've indicated. But I respect Barry's right to his opinion, and I certainly have delivered some of my own that were very critical of Padre management.

I get paid by the Padres for my work on the radio network, but that doesn't alter my willingness to be critical when I'm doing my TV shows. Several years ago I did a broad-ranging commentary in which I chastised the management of several San Diego teams, including the Padres, Chargers, and Clippers, along with San Diego State. I criticized the Padres for losing Dave Winfield with no compensation after the 1980 season. In my view, they should have traded him for a front-line player or players. In the same commentary, I was even more critical of the Clippers' Don Sterling, and I went after Aztec athletic director Gene Bourdet for changing the colors of the team's uniforms.

When I delivered this commentary, Ballard Smith was out of town skiing, but when he returned and was informed of it, he must have thought I was singling out Padre management. He called our station manager, Bob Myers, and said he didn't see how the team could use me any longer as one of its announcers. We wound up having lunch at Lubach's and clearing the air, but I'm sure Ballard has been mad at me numerous times since that incident. I think he realizes that in the long run my opinionated style gets people interested in the ball club.

There was a game in St. Louis when George Hendrick of the Cardinals trotted lazily to first base after hitting a ground ball. I was announcing the game on KFMB radio, and to underscore my impression of Hendrick's canine behavior, I barked into the microphone. Several innings later, the Padres' Garry Templeton hit into a double play and didn't exert himself running down the line to first. Failing to hustle could make the difference in a close game, and I said so. Later, I got a call from Ballard, asking me to go easy on Templeton, who had well-publicized problems with depression when he was with the Cardinals. The Padres had traded their most popular player, Ozzie Smith, to get Templeton, and I think they were still concerned about how he was going to fit in. Three years have passed, and I still don't think it was such a masterful trade, but I do believe Garry has fit in and made a big contribution. He hasn't hit over .300 as he did in St. Louis, but he's very popular with his teammates and has become a real leader. The point I want to make is that I have never pulled a punch with the Padres, or any other San Diego team, whether I've been on their payroll or not. To any of my critics, I can justify working for the Padres by pointing to my record. Enough said.

CHAPTER 14

No Tolerance for Greenflies

When the history of the Padres is written, a substantial chapter will have to be devoted to the voice of the Padres, Jerry Coleman. He's probably best known for his bloopers and malaprops, which are quite funny and are locally known as Colemanisms. But the salient fact is that Jerry is the most popular sportscaster in San Diego, bar none. I don't think anyone can touch him after the team's success in 1984.

I always get the impression that even though he laughs along with the Colemanisms whenever they're mentioned, he isn't particularly fond of hearing them brought up. He'll make reference to them on the air, but there are other topics that please him more. For those of you who may be new to the subject of Colemanisms — perhaps you just arrived from the North Woods of Maine — here are a few examples. In a 1979 broadcast, Jerry said, "Tucker Ashford slides into second with a standup double." Get the idea? On another broadcast, he said, "A high fly ball to right field . . . Winfield going back, going back; he hits his head on the wall . . . it's rolling toward second base." Or how about his comments during a pregame show dedicated to drug abuse:

"Hats off to drug abusers everywhere." I still don't believe the next one is true, but Padre producer Tommy Jorgenson swears it is, and he was there. From the opening of a broadcast at San Francisco's Candlestick Park: "Good afternoon, everyone, it's Padre baseball, the Padres against the Giants here at Candlestick. A really cold day on the bay. Look, out in centerfield, the fags are really blowing."

I think the rage over Colemanisms made people like and identify with Jerry. It showed him as a human being subject to mistakes like the rest of us — someone the audience could relate to as more than just another former ballplayer turned broadcaster. I've made numerous public appearances with Jerry, and audiences love him.

The modern-day whining, spoiled jocks should examine Jerry's life and career. He passed up a chance to get an education and play baseball on an athletic scholarship at USC in order to enlist as a fighter pilot during World War II. Later, after being named the American League Rookie of the Year in 1949 as a second baseman for the New York Yankees, he interrupted his career again to fly combat missions in the Korean War. You might hear Dave Campbell refer to a bit of baseball history that happened "while Jerry was out winning the war." Dave kids Jerry, but he has total respect for his broadcast partner, as do I. Jerry is a man's man, and many of today's ballplayers would do well to learn from him.

Aside from Jerry's popularity and his occasional slips of the tongue, another intriguing aspect of his long association with the Padres is the year he spent as manager, 1980. I think the experience really weighed on Jerry and strained his nerves. He could have used a lot of support from the players, but unfortunately he had a very unsupportive group that year. Jerry was a pretty frenetic manager, always up and moving about on the bench, and I guess he drove some of the players a little crazy. But they should have looked at his nervous energy as enthusiasm for baseball and redoubled their desire to play hard for him. Intead, many players took the opposite approach. They seemed to view him as an old man, a dumb broadcaster out of touch with baseball. They never really played for him, and that angered me, as I'm sure it did Jerry.

Jerry made his mistakes as manager, but he could have overcome some of them more readily if he'd enjoyed the backing of players like Rollie Fingers, Gene Tenace, and Ruppert Jones, who never were behind him. It could have been a fairly decent club, with Dave Winfield providing power, plus three guys who stole over 50 bases — Gene Richards, Jerry Mumphrey, and Ozzie Smith. I really thought if those guys had busted their butts for Jerry, he might still be the manager. The Padre organization gave him a chance, but the players didn't.

What really sticks in my craw is the way Fingers, the great relief pitcher, made Jerry's life miserable. Rollie is nearing the end now of a career distinguished by two things: officially, he's recorded more saves than any pitcher in baseball history, and unofficially, he's done more bitching than any ballplayer of his generation. San Diego television watchers always say anchorman Marty Levine and I are too whiny and negative. It's really too bad we couldn't have Fingers to do the weather. He would make us both seem like Mary Poppins. Nothing and no one was immune from Rollie's moaning. I was talking once with Hudson and Bauer about those three-hole, pitch 'n putt golf things, and the line was that if Rollie bought a franchise, they could name it Pitch 'N Bitch. We did some great takeoffs on Fingers, whining, "Rolllllleeeee!"

I find it difficult, regardless of how much fun I had at his expense, to forgive Fingers for the way he treated Jerry on a memorable afternoon when the manager went to the mound. Fingers was having trouble getting the side out, and in his frustration, he kicked the ground as Jerry stood there. Rollie said he wanted to be taken out, so Jerry put up his left hand, signalling the bullpen he wanted a left-hander. Then Rollie contradicted what he had just told Jerry, claiming he was OK and wanted to stay on the mound. But Jerry had already waved to the bullpen and there was no way he would be permitted to change. Whatever the reason for the breakdown in communications, Fingers should have left the mound gracefully. Instead, he stormed off, drew back his arm and threw his glove as he reached the dugout, then headed for the locker room, where he proceeded to have a fit. Later he criticized Jerry in the media. His entire act that day was unnecessary and hard to forgive.

I was hard on Fingers for that explosion, but despite that, I always had a fairly friendly relationship with him. I should amend that to "friendly in an awkward sort of way." I remember an occasion when I was flying to Yuma to announce a spring training game. Rollie, who had come back to San Diego to take care of some personal business, happened to be booked on the same flight. This was on Imperial Airlines, so we aren't talking 747. The plane was so small, there was no bathroom and no stewardesses. On board the twin-engine Cessna were the pilot and copilot, plus Rollie and me. Naturally, he and I were seated side by side. En route to Yuma, we had to land in El Centro. I'd been teasing and criticizing him on both radio and TV, so I'm certain Fingers could not have been thrilled to be stuck sitting with me. To his credit, he was cordial as we attempted to maintain a little chitchat.

Fingers was the ringleader of one of the most incredible groups of bitchers I have ever heard. Fingers, Tenace, Randy Jones, and Eric Rasmussen would just bitch up a storm. One of their favorite targets was the bus driver taking the team from an airport to a hotel or a stadium, in whatever city we happened to be visiting. It was always a derogatory form of kidding. "C'mon, bussey, turn up the goddam air conditioning. Jesus Christ!" I halfway expected one of those drivers to get out of his seat, march to the rear of the bus, and wallop one of those complainers, but it never happened.

Heaven forbid that a bus should be five minutes off the time printed on the team's itinerary. The players must have thought they were a traveling party associated with the White House. One day we were in New York and heading back into Manhattan after a losing effort against the Mets at Shea Stadium in which Fingers had suffered the defeat. As we passed an enormous cemetery, John (Doc) Mattei, the team's traveling secretary, a man with a deep, rumbling voice and a sharp wit, broke up the bus by yelling, "Hey, Fingers! See that cemetery. That's where your arm is buried." Ballplayers, lacking the mental capacity of rocket scientists, thought this was hilarious.

Today's Padres are generally easier to be around on the road, even if a lot of them don't care for me. There are two busses now, one for the bourgeoisie (the athletes) and the other for the underlings (the media and others). The players insisted on separation from the riff-raff, like writers, broadcasters, and whatever fans hap-

pened to be along as part of a promotional deal. One of
the sillier moments of 1984 happened when pitcher Greg
Booker, a rookie who'd been in the big leagues for
several weeks and whose father-in-law happens to be
Jack McKeon, was complaining because his wife had to
ride on the second bus. We're talking about a guy who
should have been thrilled beyond words just to be in the
big leagues, and here he was griping like a seasoned
veteran. It was like he thought somebody might actually
recognize Mrs. Booker and give her a difficult time.

The players have a very condescending name for
fans. They call them "greenflies." They don't want
greenflies buzzing around them like pests that should be
swatted. And Booker was complaining about his poor
wife having to be on the same bus with the greenflies,
the devoted fans who paid their own way to worship the
ballplayers. Incredible! Perhaps that gives you a little insight into why us media types get jaded after being
around ballplayers for years. They need someone to
pick on them occasionally and remind them they're not
truly the exalted of the earth.

I have to admit it was more fun traveling with the
Padres of several years ago. I got along better with
them. Very few of them refused to talk to me, or at least
nod when they passed me in the aisle. Even Dave Winfield and I got along.

I still don't know what went wrong with Winfield.
He often thanked me for my commentaries, especially
when I urged the San Diego fans to stuff the ballot box
in support of him the way fans in New York, Boston,
and other places back their local heroes. Dave had a
great arm, he could hit with power, and I never saw
anybody go from first to third as swiftly and aggressive-
ly as he did. Dave was and is a physical paragon, such a

113

magnificent long, lean, strong and supple body. I was one of his greatest fans.

A lot of players, however, didn't like Winfield. Chief among his detractors was Ozzie Smith, who came within a hair's width of hating Dave. Ozzie and several others would sing a little ditty they made up, to the tune of Old McDonald: "Ole McWinnie had a team, Me-I, Me-I, O." He was admittedly a very egotistical guy, not a leader in the fashion of Pete Rose.

Winfield and I got along until well into the 1980 season when his agent, Al Frohman, was negotiating with the Padres and discussing some very hefty numbers. I was having some fun with the topic on the Hudson and Bauer show. This was at a time when Congress was debating a tax on windfall profits enjoyed by oil companies. When Dave had a bad day, we couldn't resist doing a takeoff on the Winfield profit tax. I really didn't think any player was worth $2 million a year, but if any player was, it was Dave. Frohman must have misconstrued the essence of my views, because our relationship began to cool.

Late in the year in a game at Pittsburgh, I was called upon to fill in as host of the Randy Jones pregame TV show. Randy had controlled who had been on the air all year, and they had usually been his buddies. Guys like Winfield, Smith, Mumphrey and Von Joshua probably were not on as often as they should have been. To try to make at least partial amends, I approached Dave on this day at Three Rivers Stadium. "Nope," he said, "you're too late." I don't know if he was mad at me or at Randy, or at both of us.

As far as the subject of racism is concerned, I have never really encountered it blatantly in covering San Diego teams, but anybody who denies it exists in sports is a true dummy. Some of these athletes are from the heart of the Deep South, so they are going to have certain attitudes toward race relations. A team consists of many diverse elements, and there's no question the rednecks stick together, as do the blacks and the God-squadders. In any randomly selected group of 25 to 40 persons, you're likely to have several racists, a couple of homosexuals, and a couple of anti-Semites. It's no different on any team in any sport. I have always accepted and understood this as a fact of life. I don't think the issue of race often causes a lack of teamwork or unity. Take the New York Knicks basketball team of the early 1970s, featuring Bill Bradley and Dave DeBusschere, Willie Reed and Walt Frazier. The joke was that the 12 members of that team could go into a coffee shop and each would sit at a separate table. Unless the lack of harmony erupts into open brawling and craziness, I don't see that having a lot of individuality makes much difference. And even in extreme cases, such as the Yankee teams with Reggie Jackson and Thurman Munson, the divisiveness was more a by-product of the owner, George Steinbrenner, and the manager, Billy Martin.

What I thought was truly unfortunate during the time Winfield was negotiating with the Padres was that several other players (who happened to be black) were not performing well, and I was obliged to criticize them accordingly. You had Gene Richards playing left field like Stevie Wonder and Jerry Turner playing right like Ray Charles, and it probably appeared that I was picking on all the black players. Truthfully, color had absolutely nothing to do with it. Poor play had everything to do with it.

There was a day when a caller on my radio talk show was offering his view on the Winfield situation.

"Go ahead, Winfield, leave San Diego," the caller said. "We'll just go with Jerry Turner and there will be no difference." To which I replied, "Sir, if you're going to enter a Volkswagen in the Indy 500, you had better know a helluva shortcut. If you're talking about replacing Dave Winfield with Jerry Turner, this conversation is over."

I know word of that show got back to Turner, because the next week, when we were in Cincinnati, I happened to pass Jerry in the tunnel leading from the field to the locker room. Now Jerry wasn't going to make anybody's list of great conversationalists. In fact, he had been on a postgame show with Bob Chandler and in response to a question, he just sat there and nodded, like a short Moses Malone. But Jerry and I had always been on pleasant terms. As we reached the clubhouse, I put my hand on his shoulder to let him enter first. "Look, man," he said gruffly, "keep your hands off me." Then he let me know what he thought of my Volkswagen analogy. He stood there cursing and saying, "Fuckin' Volkswagen, huh? Fuckin' Volkswagen."

I tried to explain that, in my honest opinion, there was no way to compare a Jerry Turner with a talent such as Dave Winfield. But he just stalked off, cursing. If I had any problem with the blacks of that era, it was only because they were undistinguished players. One of the more lamentable plays I ever saw by a big leaguer involved Turner. It happened in St. Louis. Turner was in left field that day. When Lou Brock sliced a hit to left, Turner fielded the ball and somehow threw it behind him in an attempt to get it to the relay man. I assume he was going to throw to second and in mid-throw, changed his mind and tried to hit the cutoff man. He wound up short-arming it and the ball went behind him, as Brock circled the bases.

CHAPTER 15

One Care Package Needed

I've been associated with a lot of teams as a play-by-play or color man, beginning with Oklahoma State and Oklahoma University, then continuing with the Hartford Whalers, Philadelphia Eagles, San Diego Padres and Clippers. But never have I seen an organization that ranked lower, in terms of efficient management, than the San Diego Chargers in the Gene Klein era.

I have a certain grudging respect for Gene Klein, because he started out with nothing and made himself a multimillionaire businessman. His story has its inspiring moments. He was a child of the Depression and sold newspapers on the streets of New York City. Later he was a pilot in World War II. After the war, he moved West and sold cars in the San Fernando Valley. Following that venture, he got into motion pictures and made his real fortune. With part of that fortune — roughly $10 million — he bought into the Chargers in 1966. Fifteen years later, after the Charger drug scandal and other misadventures, he sold out for $70 million. I have to tip my cap to his great business acumen. I believe, however, that he knew he had participated in the dismantling of a once-great team. And like all smart businessmen, he knew when to get out.

The question Gene Klein would have a hard time

answering, however, is this: "Did you make the world a better place to live in, or the Chargers' organization a better place to work?" I don't see how he could honestly answer "yes" to either question. The feel,the tone, the mentality of a business organization is set at the very top, and that was the case with the Chargers under Gene Klein. He had icewater in his veins, and I think that coldness extended through the whole organization. Furthermore, that cold managerial style quickly reached a point of diminishing returns. Few people in the organization were happy, even in the years when the team was winning and had the town all excited.

There was always an air of calculation during Klein's reign. I know of a philanthropic group that called the team to ask if a couple of players could appear at a charity event. A team representative asked if players from other local teams would be present. He was told, "yes," players from the Sockers and Padres would also be there. "Well," the Charger man replied, "if we're not going to be the focal point, we're not going to be involved." That was typical of how the Chargers operated for far too long. Why bother to help some crippled children if the Chargers couldn't get the main public relations benefit?

Until I got to know the Chargers, I had never seen a team that, from top to bottom, just didn't care what anyone outside the organization thought. A friend of mine produced a weekly TV show on the team back in the mid-1970s. The team was playing badly then, but he tells me their attitude was the same then as it is now. Even when they could have used some help peddling tickets, they seemed to think you were imposing on them by asking for an interview or two. They have long treated the media as if the Chargers were performing a big service merely by answering the telephone. I give them credit for consistency, if nothing else. They didn't just become assholes when they emerged as the Super Chargers.

They're on the downswing again. Regardless, they still maintain the stance that they don't give a damn about anybody. I can honestly say, with no animosity, they are the most amazing franchise in sports in this regard. Maybe this will change under Alex Spanos. I don't think he deserves to be included in my indictment yet. I hope he'll work to change the organization's attitude.

The rise and fall of the Chargers under Gene Klein is a familiar story to San Diegans. He took a team that was the dregs of the league and made it a powerhouse for five years, and then it all went sour on him. In the mid-70s, he did a terrific job of hiring people, and he had a fantastic draft in 1975, when Louie Kelcher and Gary Johnson and several others arrived to form the nucleus of the great teams to come. In 1978 he got rid of Tommy Prothro and hired Don Coryell as coach, which was a smart public relations stroke because of Don's San Diego State connections. Then, after fashioning one of the great offensive attacks in football history, they just began doing everything wrong. They blew it. An analogous situation is the Texas Longhorns under Darrell Royal, whose Wishbone offense was once strides ahead of the defenses. When Chuck Fairbanks was at Oklahoma, Texas beat the team 49-7, so he installed the Wishbone the next week. He called his players together and issued a warning to the world, "If anybody wants to beat us, they better hurry up and do it." And he was right. Oklahoma became unbeatable and stayed that way for the better part of a decade.

The Chargers' offensive philosophy was so inventive, it has rightly been called the stuff of genius. Whether it was the work of Joe Gibbs, who later became the head coach of the Washington Redskins, or whether it was Coryell's inspiration alone, the Chargers were so far ahead of the defenses that conventional 4-3 setups were just blown away. But at the same time they were reveling in the exploits of Dan Fouts, Kellen Winslow, John Jefferson, and company, they were just criminally neglecting the defense. I once heard John Brodie say on an NBC telecast that the Charger defense was as bad as any he had seen in the NFL in a decade. But the team's response was no response. Take the 1981 draft, when their first choice was a 5'9" running back named James Brooks. They put forth their usual simplistic nonsense about taking the best available athlete. What the hell good is a 5'9" runner when you don't have a pass rush or a secondary?

Call it folly or whatever, but the Chargers just kept drafting tight ends and quarterbacks and wide receivers over the years, even while the defense was falling apart. I'm afraid I have to assign Don Coryell a lot of the blame. When he was in St. Louis, he criticized Cardinal owner, Bill Bidwill, because he wasn't allowed an active role in the draft. A coach should be involved. And Coryell obviously was involved in the Chargers' draft — but his offensive orientation was allowed to manifest itself in spite of obvious defensive shortcomings the club had.

The Chargers had this little game they played with the fans year after year. They would draft a defender on the seventh round and come out with a statement like, "We couldn't believe he was still available. We had him listed higher." So what if he had two bad knees and had broken his ankle his sophomore year? They expected the fans and the media to fall for that kind of deception.

I frankly don't know how they expected to keep winning. Not only did they draft poorly, they also traded poorly. The really sad thing is that, not so long ago, they had some pretty darned tough defensive linemen. The 1979 and 1980 defensive lines featured Fred Dean, Louie Kelcher, Leroy Jones, and Gary Johnson, plus some fairly decent linebackers. But it all started to unravel when they traded Fred Dean to San Francisco in 1981 following a contract dispute.

Now to give Gene Klein his due, I'm willing to acknowledge that Dean was involved in some less than exemplary off-the-field activities, and they continued after he went to the 49ers. He asked to renegotiate his San Diego contract, and he pulled the same thing with Ed DeBartolo a few years later in San Francisco. He wound up with a fat new contract and proved he could still play, but he also proved to be a pain in the neck to the management in both cities. Having said that, I also have to acknowledge that Fred is the best pass rusher on the planet, and perhaps an owner should bend over backward to accommodate his whims. Even if he'd been a model citizen, Dean would have had no future here because Gene Klein wasn't going to allow any player to tell him what to do. He was the boss and he had a policy of never renegotiating a contract.

If I were an owner, I would say to the ballplayers, "Look, this is football's top pass rusher. Just because I reward him for excellence, that doesn't mean I'm going to do it for the fortieth man on the roster. You fellows can all line up and ask for money, but you don't get it until you produce as Fred Dean has done." The irony is that the Chargers signed Dean for a song when he was a rookie, just as they did so many others. These guys were naive and had no big reputations to command a lucrative contract.

It was pretty much the same story with John Jefferson, the talented and ultrapopular wide receiver who likewise sought to renegotiate a contract that had left him dramatically underpaid. The fact that Gene Klein sent Jefferson to Green Bay was no accident. He would have traded JJ to Alaska if there had been a franchise up there. It was a message to all the players: don't mess with Gene Klein, or you, too, will be freezing your ass off. Gene showed he was tough, but I don't think he came off looking too shrewd.

The Chargers were never the same after Jefferson left. Not in esprit de corps. Sure, they kept scoring the points and winning occassional games 49–39. But his departure took the heart out of the team. It made players like Kellen Winslow very unhappy. Right after the JJ deal, the players even boycotted a team banquet, sending Mr. Klein a message that I don't think really registered. It was counterproductive to trade Jefferson, even though Gene had already made some financial adjustments as a favor to him the year before.

Hey, nobody dragged Gene Klein into the football business. He's got to realize players have a very short career and they've got to capitalize while they can. They can easily get in over their heads when they negotiate their first contracts. Management should be more responsive when the players later want to rectify earlier errors. I certainly don't blame a player for trying to maximize his income after the ball club has stuck it to him on what they euphemistically refer to as "a series of one-year contracts" signed fresh out of college.

John Jefferson was a phenomenon in this town. He would come onto the field waving a towel and dancing, and the stadium would go bonkers. The opposing team was dead before the opening kickoff. All that left with JJ. It's not the same anymore. Not remotely close, even for a Raiders' game. When JJ packed his Samsonites, the heart and soul of the Chargers went with him. Those are rare commodities in pro sports. You don't part with them lightly. I don't think Gene Klein even gave Jefferson's value a second thought. He just blew it.

While the Charger offense struggled to keep up with the flurry of points being given away by the defense, fans were picking on San Diego defensive coaches. And unfairly, in my opinion. I've never put much of the blame on defensive coordinator Jack Pardee, who was here for one year, or Tom Bass, who's been in charge since 1982. Pardee certainly made some mistakes, such as trying to make the personnel conform to his system, instead of the other way around. Many of the players at his disposal simply didn't have the tools to do it the way he wanted it done. The results haven't been noticeably better under Bass, but at least he's been more open-minded about what he's tried to do. There's a saying in the news business: "It may be a slow news day, but you still have to fill an hour of air time." Bass has to field a defensive team, even though it's been a slow news day ever since his arrival. You could put George Halas or Vince Lombardi or Mrs. Tom Bass in charge of the San Diego defense, and it wouldn't make much difference, given the material that's been available over the last three or four years.

When I give a speech, I have a standard line that goes, "See that empty table in the back. Good to see all the Charger defensive All-Pros could make it tonight." I ask my audience to pretend they have an expansion franchise to stock. Suppose they could have any player off the Charger defense. Who would it be? The typical response is silence. The defense rests.

It simply isn't fair to come down on the Charger defensive coaches when they're working with seventh-round draft choices and rejects from other teams and the USFL. The blame rests on the shoulders of Gene Klein, John Sanders, and Don Coryell. They let the defense go to hell. They're responsible for the current mess. The Chargers were, without question, the strongest team in the AFC West from 1979 through 1981. Now, just four years later, they're possibly the worst. Even Kansas City has moved past them. Hell, the Chargers don't even have the receivers anymore. I would rather have the Chiefs' receivers, Carlos Carson, Anthony Hancock, Stephone Paige, and Henry Marshall. Even the strength of the team is no longer the great asset it once was.

Some critics have gone after the new owner, Alex Spanos, for failing to retain Ed Luther as backup quarterback to Dan Fouts. In this case, I believe the Chargers did the correct thing. Ed Luther was simply not worth the $650,000 a year he got from the USFL. His agent, Leigh Steinberg, said Luther was the best number two quarterback in the league, which sounded reassuring until Dan Fouts was hurt and Luther got the chance to start. He demonstrated that he couldn't read defenses and that he couldn't get the job done. He won only two of nine games when Dan was hurt, numbers that speak volumes. Of course, the Chargers are still in precarious shape entering the 1985 season with Bruce Mathison as the principal backup to Fouts.

Incidentally, it's no coincidence that the Chargers experienced two straight losing seasons when Fouts was down for extended periods. Dan is in his middle thirties now, but he remains a great quarterback, one destined for the Hall of Fame. He also remains the unquestioned leader of the team. Well, almost unquestioned. Never the most popular guy, he got into a shouting match with Rolf Benirschke during a game in 1984. If you can't get along with Rolf, something is wrong with you.

Looking back at the time when Fouts was really starting to establish himself, his teammates voted John Jefferson the most valuable player on the Chargers. Dan should have had that honor, in my opinion, but he simply wasn't as well liked as JJ. I once asked Dan if he thought the voting went along racial lines, but he wouldn't answer. Fact is, many players, then and now, believe Dan is arrogant and egotistical. He's a true leader and a gutsy player, and he has his moments of keen insight. The morning after Luther went to the USFL, Hudson and Bauer placed a call to his house in Sisters, Oregon. The connection was bad, and they told Dan they would call back. When the second call went through, H & B neglected to tell No. 14 he was on the air. There followed a question about an upcoming bowling tournament for charity. "Who gives a shit, anyway?" Dan said.

I've had my differences with Dan, but they seem minor compared to my running feud with tight end Kellen Winslow. I don't hate Kellen, as people must think, but he may feel that way about me — I can't speak for Kellen. The first shot was fired in 1978 when I was broadcasting San Diego State football games. There was a game at Missouri, Kellen's alma mater. The first three quarters, it was all Aztecs. Kellen was listening and thinking I sounded like a jerk because his team was losing. Later he leveled some criticism at my performance in the papers. I thought he should have been paying more attention to learning his job, which at the time was as a rookie tight end. The peace pipe really wasn't shared until five years later, when I "bought" his friendship. That is, KFMB hired him as Hank Bauer's replacement as the analyst on our 5 p.m. newscast during the football season. For $600 a week or so, Kellen became my buddy. If that's all it takes, I wish the station would buy Gossage, Nettles, Templeton, Wiggins, Thurmond, and all the others who think I'm less than swell.

I really do hope Kellen will make a comeback from the knee injury he suffered in 1984. But it appears to be a longshot as this is written. According to the doctors, he faces the possibility of not being able to walk again if he somehow reinjures the knee. That's some hard choice for anyone to have to make.

Fouts and Winslow have never been on my list of all-time favorites, but without hesitating I would put Louie Kelcher near the top. He was a sort of Tim Flannery in shoulder pads. Once, when my car was broken into and all my Willie Nelson tapes were stolen, I went on the air and said, "If the slimy parasite who broke into my car is listening, it's OK that you took my radio and smashed my rear window. But for taking my Willie Nelson tapes, I will surely track you down and kill you!" A week later, as I was driving out of the stadium parking lot after a Padre game, Kelcher pulled up beside me, rolled down his window, and yelled, "Hey, Ted! Thanks for the Willie Nelson tapes!"

CHAPTER 16

Smallfry

Now that we've cleared the air about the Chargers, I'd like to make one teeny qualification. Earlier I said the Chargers were the most incredibly mismanaged team I ever saw. But in fairness I would have to include the San Diego Clippers as co-defendant in this indictment. Make that the Los Angeles Clippers. Their owner, Donald Sterling, deserves a book of his own. He single-handedly destroyed pro basketball in this town, what there was of it. Pro basketball never really had a chance to make it on its own merits in San Diego, and consequently it never did well at the gate. Sterling saw to it that we will probably never get another franchise in this century. So poorly run was the franchise — and the Sports Arena along with it — that I'm sure the National Basketball Association will never make another move in our direction. And that's a shame, because I believe the NBA could have succeeded here. San Diego is no different from any other city — it demands a winner and a class act, or at least a semi-class act. The only year the fans had a decent team, 1978, they backed it pretty well. Attendance averaged nearly 9,000 that first season the Clippers were here. I know Al McGuire said basketball could never thrive in a town where you could hear the tinkle of the bells on the sailboats all winter long, and that's a hell of a point. Basketball is biggest in climates where there's not much entertainment competition in the winter. But, conceding that, I still believe the NBA could make it here, given half a chance.

Donald T. Sterling has to be the greatest buffoon ever to masquerade as a franchise owner in pro sports. Here was a guy who made mega-millions in real estate, and knew nothing about basketball, or athletics in general for that matter. He just wanted a sweaty plaything to make him "somebody" in the eyes of his Beverly Hills and Malibu playmates. After doing everything wrong, he then turned around and blamed the city of San Diego. He bought the team from Irv Levin in 1981, proclaiming his great love for San Diego. He immediately got off to a bad start by plastering his picture on buses and billboards all over San Diego County. He should have been selling basketball or basketball players, not his anemic smile.

I doubt that he ever intended to keep the team in San Diego. He was going to take it to L. A. where he could sip Perrier or white wine with his buddies, and never mind what it meant to San Diego's basketball future. I don't think I have ever seen a greater display of malicious stupidity than the time he called a press conference and announced he wanted the team to finish last so it could draft first. That earned him a $10,000 fine from the league, which was richly deserved. Of course, his response was to blame the media. I said he was dumb, but he wasn't a slow learner. He learned that response from the athletes real quickly.

As much blame as Don Sterling deserves for the demise of pro basketball here, the death knell actually sounded when Irv Levin signed Bill Walton to a five-year contract back in 1979. That was an enormous risk

Levin took, gambling on Bill's health, and it blew up in his face. Bill was never going to be himself again, and the club never had a winning season with him on the roster. There were many other blunders, such as trading the enormously popular Lloyd (World) Free and hiring a rookie coach, Paul Silas. When you look back at it, there wasn't much this organization ever did right.

I did some radio and TV work for the Clippers, but that didn't stop me from telling the sorry truth about the team all along. Irv Kaze, who used to be in the Clipper front office, bitched about me from time to time. I once said World Free was going to file for free agency if the Clippers didn't offer him a better contract. Irv proceeded to claim that I put the idea in Free's head, which was utter nonsense. After all, World's agent, Fred Slaughter, was capable of figuring the options for himself. There was no way to please Irv, who insisted that something lame like wristband night be promoted over and over. We used to kid about having to do a promo for Marvin Barnes Tire-Iron Night. No matter how hard an announcer pumped, Kaze wanted more plugs. He never wanted the game to interfere with the promotions.

To their credit, the Clippers never yanked the plug on me. I was critical of Levin and Sterling from the start, and I never stopped. Maybe they figured I'd be even more critical if they canned me. I made $10,000 in 1983 for broadcasting 15 Clipper games on TV. I never talked to Sterling much; we just avoided each other. I knew he didn't like me, but I didn't pull back. I have no apologies to make to my viewers. I only regret that they were screwed so badly by the management of the Clippers over the years.

I'm happy to report that indoor soccer fans have experienced a better fate than their basketball counterparts. It appears the indoor game is here to stay. The game is often compared to hockey, but it's different in one important respect. You can see what happens when a goal is scored. In hockey you just can't see the damn puck, particularly on TV. In soccer, the ball is pretty hard to miss.

Soccer is a good, fast-paced game with enough scoring to keep the fans interested and entertained. All of my comments here, keep in mind, pertain to indoor soccer, not outdoor. The purists will have to look elsewhere if they want something on their sport. I really believe soccer is destined to get a television contract from a cable network, and that will eventually guarantee the league's future. To be truthful, the league doesn't require a lot of subsistence money. The players are getting hosed down by the owners because their union really sold them down the river. They accepted a salary cap on top of the already minuscule salaries they're receiving. In effect the owners said to the players, "We have you in poverty. Now we want you to sign a contract that will keep you there for the rest of your careers." A superstar like Steve Zungul gets his $200,000, but the rest are getting $30,000 or so. What a tremendous deal for ownership.

The payoff from a championship season is about $1,800 per man for the Sockers. Compare that to baseball, where the Padres received $40,000 or so for losing the World Series. Winning a Super Bowl is worth $75,000. During the 1984 season, while the Sockers were in a midseason slump, I went on TV after Julie Veee scored four goals in a game, and I said, "You can always tell when the playoffs are coming and the money is on the line. Julie can smell the money." A few minutes later I received a call from, guess who, Julie Veee. "What's this money stuff?" he demanded indignantly. "I made $500 from the playoffs last year." That was a real shock to me. The arenas were all filled for the playoffs, so owners like Bob Bell had to be pocketing some money. What the players receive would barely equal the meal money baseball players get on a two-week trip.

The way it's set up, the league just can't fold. The owners would have to get together and toss their capital on a bonfire. What a sweet deal! The players have no choice but to accept what's offered. Most of them are not quite good enough to make it in the European leagues, so they have nowhere else to turn.

I am happy to see the Sockers succeeding, but I wish they'd cut some of the hype. It's beneath them. I mean, they turn on the twirling lights and the smoke, and you think you've entered a French whorehouse. Then the announcer gives you the big, "Julie Veeeeeeeeeee!" It's embarrassing for me to sit through a game. I'd rather drive a truck than listen to the honker who handles the Sockers microphone. I've told Bob Bell they should cut the crap, but he doesn't listen. I also wish the players would stop kissing and hugging so much. Why there's no San Francisco franchise in soccer is beyond me.

While pro basketball is dead and soccer thrives in San Diego, I'm not sure what the score is with college athletics. San Diego State has been making noises about the possibility of having to go back to Division II, for financial reasons. If they do that, they might as well close the doors. You can't go home again. They were successful under Don Coryell as a Division II football power, but then they tried the big time, and it hasn't worked out as planned. If they go back to playing Cal Poly and Long Beach State, the next sound you hear will be a collective yawn. I'd hate to be in the shoes of Mary Alice Hill, the Aztec athletic director.

People love to be associated with a winner, so the chemistry was there in the Coryell era. It didn't matter that they weren't playing UCLA and Missouri. In the old days San Diego State kept everybody happy simply by winning. When they decided to step up into the big leagues, they did it wrong on a couple of fronts. First of all, they joined the Western Athletic Conference when they should have been lobbying to get into the Pac 10. They should have gone for the glamour schools and the big guarantees. The WAC had no attraction, except Brigham Young University. When some team like New Mexico came to San Diego, there was simply no draw. There is no other WAC team in California, no other natural rivalry. There's no team with marquee value. So when the Aztecs thought they were going big time, they really weren't.

There were other mistakes, too. When Gene Bourdet was the athletic director, he changed the uniforms from black to red, which outraged the tradition-minded alumni. They changed the ticket priorities and the starting times of the games, which had always been played at night so people could get out and do something in the sun during the day. These moves likewise met with disfavor. Still another grave error was firing popular coach Claude Gilbert one year after he had an 8-3 record in 1979.

The sad truth is that the Pac 10 doesn't need or want San Diego State, which doesn't exactly bode well for the future of the school's athletic program. Even if the Aztecs had, or have, no chance to enter the Pac 10, they might have been able to make a go of it as an independent. The theory would be to play name schools, take your lumps, and build your program a little. Either that, or remain Division II, where they were winning and drawing good crowds.

I believe head football coach Doug Scovil is a real student of the game. He's a very professorial guy that any pro team would like to have as its offensive coordinator. But I don't know if he's the ideal guy to be head coach. He seems to be more a man who should be minding the game plan while someone else takes care of the motivating and recruiting. A football coach, you have to remember, has a greater impact on the game than his counterpart in baseball or basketball. There's so much emotion in football, and the coach has to be able to tap that, and direct it. A team can beat a better opponent if it has the right motivation. I really don't know if Doug Scovil is the type to perform that function. He's too low-key. A great history professor doesn't necessarily make a great university president, and I don't think the great offensive mind automatically makes a great head coach.

Aside from the need to get the players frothing at the mouth, a coach is responsible for getting good players into the program. Recruiting requires charisma. A great coach needs that, and he needs to be able to gladhand the alumni and assert himself in the community as a personality. He has to be able to draw some laughs, put everyone in the spirit. He has to get people excited, because there's nobody else there to do it. If he can't get people excited, it makes the job of raising money that much tougher. The jury is very much out on whether Doug has the necessary qualities as motivator, charmer, and snake oil salesman.

Smokey Gaines, the Aztec basketball coach, is everything Doug Scovil is not. Most people feel Doug is a terrific strategist, while they tend to give Smokey low marks for his performance as a game coach. But Smokey can recruit with the best of 'em. He can tell stories and charm people with his personality.

I was out one night with Smokey when he told a cocktail waitress he wanted some exotic drink, like a sloe gin fizz. She said they didn't have that particular drink. Just putting her on, Smokey said, "I knew it. I had it figured when I walked in here. You don't serve blacks do you?" The woman, seemingly mortified, apologized profusely and assured him they did indeed serve blacks. "Awright," Smokey said, "I want three of them. A 6'10" center and two 6'9" forwards." The paralyzed waitress didn't even realize it was a joke.

Despite the conventional wisdom, I happen to think Smokey can coach. It's long been said he could speak the language of the inner city and get kids to come to San Diego State, but that seems simplistic. I don't want to perpetuate a myth here. I thought the coaching job he did in the 1984-85 season proved once and for all he's a very competent coach. This was no dream team, but it won 23 games and was invited to the NCAA tournament. Granted, it was a down year for teams like BYU and New Mexico, but Smokey still did a fine job of getting the best out of the talent at his disposal, and that's all any coach can be asked to do.

The larger issue, of course, is whether the Aztecs can make it at the Division I level. I'm inclined to say, "no." They simply don't have the money. I look at the back of the football program where the top contributors are listed. Top dollar in this supposedly elite group is $10,000. That wouldn't get you in line to buy tickets at places like Oklahoma. George Lukas gave $1 million to the USC film department because that's where he got his start, and you compare that to $10,000 donations to

Aztec athletics. Draw your own conclusions. It seems the wealthiest alumnnus the Aztecs can tap is some car dealer who parts with ten grand, and they think, "Whoopteedoo." Where are the rich bigshots from San Diego State? They can't all be boosting UCLA. San Diego State can't even raise the dough to build a fieldhouse. Their present arena, Peterson Gym, wouldn't accommodate some of the larger high schools. Until someone like Joan Kroc writes a check for $1 million to get the ball rolling in the form of seed money, they won't even have a suitable gym. The hard fact is, you've got to have the juice. You can't be stuck raising $50 and $100 a donor. As long as that's the funding situation, and the WAC remains a mediocre conference with a small TV market, the numbers just don't add up to big time at San Diego State.

One last point. I was the voice of the Aztecs for four years. I've lived in and visited many college towns, and 'dis ain't one. In places like Tuscaloosa or Norman, the university *is* the town. But this is a resort area, with dozens of recreational sports and a couple of professional teams. Getting people's attention is tough. Al McGuire's line about the ding-ding-ding of the sailboats has at least as much relevance for San Diego State athletics as it did for the Clippers.

CHAPTER 17

The Pay Is Good, the Perks Are Better

Some of the best things in life are free. The rest are available to professional athletes as perks. We've talked about women, endorsements, and business opportunities. Now let's touch on the travel. I used to joke with Gene Shue, when he was coaching the Clippers. All his players rode first class, and he rode in the back (with the real people, like yours truly). "Ah, that's why they call you coach," I said. He informed me the players were guaranteed first-class seats. If there were not enough seats up front, the club was obliged to buy three coach seats for every two players. The arithmetic of that is pretty staggering: a team would spend $700 for an empty seat on the New York to San Diego connection. What a mighty union! And it's that way in baseball, too.

On top of it all, the athletes stay in the finest modern hotels. Their bags are taken care of by the club's attendants. Their plane reservations and tickets are also handled. There isn't much required in the way of mental or physical exertion, except what goes into each ball game. That adds up to roughly two hours of labor per day. Naturally, they take this luxury for granted. One time in Atlanta, the Padres requested their traveling secretary, Doc Mattei, to have newspapers sent up to their rooms so they wouldn't have to go down to the lobby and risk wrist injury signing an autograph. My God, that would wreck a player's day. And one guy didn't like the green decor of his room, so he forced a switch with a writer.

The players receive $47 a day meal money when they're traveling, and that should take care of most appetites, considering that a free meal is provided in the clubhouse after every game. It's also possible to get offers of free meals from time to time from friends, business connections, or others wanting to impress a player. As a last resort, a player can always eat at McDonald's. And believe me, some do.

What, with the cruel world closing in on them from every direction, is it any wonder that some athletes crumble when faced with the ordeal of signing an autograph. I can understand how a guy might tire of being insulted by boorish middle-aged fans, but not by an eight-year-old. As a kid I'd go to wrestling matches in Asbury Park, New Jersey and get autographs from guys like Ricky Starr and Killer Kowalski. I would stand by the ring post and hold out my paper. Real neat stuff. It doesn't matter if a kid doesn't keep the autograph for years. After all, it's just a way of showing a friend you met a famous athlete. The misfits who refuse to sign a scrap of paper for a child have lost the human touch. Yet we continue to reward some of these jerks — Bill Russell, for example — by giving them lucrative broadcasting jobs. It doesn't cost a dime to be nice, to give back a little to the public and to the sports world that lavished so much on these men.

Some retired baseball players, notably Robin Roberts, Mickey Mantle, and Bob Feller, have started charging up to $90 for a notarized autograph. At first glance, this borders on scandalous exploitation. I suppose it's because memorabilia collecting has become a cottage industry with trade shows and profiteering. Collectors make good money buying and swapping cards, programs, uniforms, and the like. The old players see a 1952 autograph going for a grand and they want a piece of the action. Maybe entrepreneurs are abusing the system. But the current players certainly should be more discriminating in their conduct.

Along with giving autographs, ballplayers should be required to be accessible for interviews for a reasonable period each day. A player refusal should result in a fine. This is a business. A bad game or one story with an inaccuracy is no excuse. It would be like me not doing my show because I made a mistake the night before. I don't label all athletes as jerks or cokeheads, and I don't treat them all the same, but the level of paranoia is stunning. The great tendency is to treat the media as a pack of hatchetmen. Baseball players are the worst. Football and basketball players seem more tolerant, and no soccer player I know of ever took a no-interview stand. I just don't know why baseball players, who have the best pay and most luxurious travel conditions, have to be so damn self important. Yet they are the loudest whiners.

A number of these guys are probably going to regret their lack of generosity when they get a little older. Us media guys will have our revenge when the jocks hit 55 or 60 years old and haven't done any interviews for 20 years. They'll yearn for a World Series with media clustered around them in droves, hanging on their every word. Perhaps a tear will come to the eye, and the player will think, "Damn, I wish I'd appreciated what I had. It was a great life."

There was a story about Mickey Mantle returning to New York for a visit long after he retired. He was staying in a lavish hotel suite with a spectacular view of New York. As he was standing by the window, the writer looked at him, and it got real quiet. Then Mantle said, "Look at that! That is some city out there. And years ago it was all mine." As a player, Mantle had been surly and hadn't handled himself well with the media. I'm sure he looks back and wishes he could still run and hit and have people rushing up for interviews. For all the nontalkers and thankless athletes, guys with the attitude, "I played three hours of baseball today for $1 million and I'm tired," I wish each of you a nice quiet room when you're 60. A quiet little room, where nobody will bother you anymore.

There are, of course, isolated instances when it's better for a coach or athlete to keep his mouth shut, as we observe in the case of a couple of college wonders, John Thompson and Bobby Knight. Their raving is hard to tolerate, even at a great distance. Thompson, the basketball coach at Georgetown, should have been a member of Hitler's staff. Like Knight, he's an intelligent guy who stresses the fundamental importance of classroom work. Then he turns around and treats basketball as if it's Pentagon-level in importance. He took his team to Hawaii for a game, and the team stayed at a hotel in Kona, 98 miles away. And that was typical road game behavior. To arrange an interview, even a high-powered organization like *Sports Illustrated* has to go through half a dozen layers of red tape. Ridiculous! These kids are not in the State Department. For their own sake, they should be learning a little about how to communicate. I remember after Georgetown won the championship in 1984 two members of the team were interviewed by Brent Musburger, and they were incapable of any utterances beyond a simple, "Well, uh, you know, you know." They even had trouble with the you-knows. It was pathetic.

No question. Thompson has got to change. After Patrick Ewing was awarded to the New York Knicks in the NBA draft lottery, there were reports Thompson had been offered a pro coaching job. That would mean a change, because his conduct certainly would not be acceptable to pro athletes.

Earlier in Ewing's senior year, Thompson brought in TV analyst Billy Packer to help the players learn the basics of conducting an interview. Thompson probably instructed him to tell the players never to reveal anything. Most athletes, Georgetown's included, seem to think the media is beneath them. On camera, a jock will look anyplace but at the interviewer. Ewing, on the day he was presented to the Knicks, possibly the most important day of his athletic career, wouldn't even grant a brief interview to CBS. Thompson did a wonderful job on him, I would say.

This thing about athletes avoiding eye contact is hard to fathom. The one exception was when Houston Rockets Coach Bill Fitch was working with rookie Akeem Olajuwon. Akeem wouldn't look his coach in the eye. His gaze was always directed at the ground. Fitch got mad and told him to look him in the eye like a man. He felt somewhat differently when Akeem told him that in Nigeria, his homeland, it was a sign of great disrespect to look a superior in the eye. That's a cultural difference you can live with, but with most American athletes, there's no excuse.

A guy like Jim Rice of the Boston Red Sox wonders why he doesn't get respect and why he's had a bad image. He once did an interview with a reporter, and during the entire course of the talk, he had his face buried in a newspaper. When someone reports that he's cold, or stares like Sonny Liston, he should examine his behavior. Al Oliver is the same way. He blames the whole world, excluding himself, for fostering the image he's not a team player, when his main preoccupation is getting 3,000 hits. He talks of how he changed positions several times during his career. Of course, the reason was that he had not mastered any position.

All of this is a roundabout way of leading up to one of the most compelling studies in sports, Bobby Knight of Indiana. Bobby is like Archie Bunker: he doesn't think he's paranoid, he just believes everybody is out to get him. Specifically, the media is after him. Following his infamous chair-throwing incident in the 1985 season, he talked of how he demands so much extra from his players, how he demands perfection both of his players and the officials in a game. Nobody is permitted a mistake in Bobby's world. Everyone must be perfect. Except Bobby. He can curse and throw chairs and embarrass his university. He can grab the players and scream in their faces, all because he believes he is striving for a perfection in them that he has yet to find in himself.

When I see a guy like Knight, I think, good heavens, there must have been someone who used to push him and berate him unmercifully and was never satisfied with anything he did. I believe Bobby Knight should consult a psychiatrist, and I'm not trying to be cute or insulting when I say that. A lot of us need help, and it's no sign of weakness to face it. Bobby is widely accepted as the best college basketball coach alive, and his former players speak very highly of him. In many respects, he does a terrific job, but he has got to learn to control his temper and his foul mouth. He should make more of an effort to control the demons that are pushing him over the brink.

Indiana state representatives were ready at one point to pass resolutions censuring him for the chair-throwing incident. When all the fallout from that happening was in the air, Bobby told his players they would have to be warriors, diving and pushing like savages. My question is, "Why? What's being a 'warrior' got to do with having your educational priorities in order?" That's the part of Bobby's psychological mix that is so confusing. Bobby wasn't that good a player. Why should his current players emulate a guy who wasn't even a starter? Coach Freud would have a lot of fun puzzling this man out.

Being a disciplinarian is fine, but I'm convinced Bobby Knight is going to punch out some kid one day and embarrass himself and his school beyond repair. He will thereby ruin what has been a truly great career. A former player, Isiah Thomas, once attended a banquet with Knight. During a question and answer period, he was asked what Coach Knight had taught him. "Oh, lots of things, like shit, son of a bitch, bastard, and asshole," Thomas said. The place was in shock. The redness must have been creeping up Knight's body from his socks to his neck. The two men didn't speak again for more than a year.

When you treat people as subhumans, it comes back to haunt you. Vince Lombardi had his moments. Jerry Kramer, the great Packers guard, described how the players hated and feared Lombardi, but also respected him. To me, it's such a waste to motivate by fear. Such a cheap way to win games. In most cases,

Lombardi got away with it. One time, however, he cussed out his quarterback, Bart Starr, in front of the entire team. Later, Starr went to him and said, "Don't you ever do that again. I can't be the leader of this team if you're going to get in my face and insult me." Lombardi must have recognized the truth of that, because he didn't insult Starr anymore.

Howard Cosell tells a story of how he had arranged to do an on-field interview with Lombardi one day. It was cleared in advance, but when Lombardi got his coaching face on, he started ranting and screaming, and he went berserk when he saw Howard's camera crew approaching. "Get that goddamn camera outta here," he screamed. "You, Cosell, get the hell out of here." Cosell saw him later, after Lombardi had settled back into his humanoid mode. Just as Bart Starr had done, Cosell asked the coach never to treat him that way again. Lombardi was apologetic, but he remained the kind of man who would insult the media just to let his players know he was tough on everybody, not just on them.

That may be masterful psychology, but there's no excuse for it in my book. There is never an excuse for screaming and cursing at a human being the way so many of our coaches and managers do. They think they can get away with it by later saying "I'm sorry." In my view, you should a treat a player with respect in all situations. If you don't mean something, don't say it. Dick Williams is very much in the mold of the taskmaster, and he certainly gets results. The players go out there to try to show him he's wrong. But surely there are better, more decent ways to get results.

CHAPTER 18

Civil Rights and Wrongs

When I was in my early teens, my hero was not Mickey Mantle or Jerry West. It was astronaut John Glenn. I attended a ticker tape parade in New York after Glenn's orbital flight in February 1962. It was a very cold day. I was standing next to a mounted policeman, and I could see the steam coming from the horse's nostrils. When the motorcade reached our spot, I ran out to the car and touched the arm of Glenn's fellow astronaut, Alan Shepard. I resolved never to wash that hand again. Later, I watched Glenn's return to his hometown in Ohio. Some guy made a speech about the feeling in the pit of his stomach, the place went nuts, and the hair was standing up on the back of my neck as I watched the TV.

I could be wrong, but I don't think kids nowadays are the same. They have heroes, sure. Heroes like Michael Jackson and Prince. Ballplayers have lost some of their heroic dimensions. I think today's ballplayers have adopted the attitude of not wanting to be heroes. They want to take their $1 million salary and be normal people, forgetting that kids still tend to emulate players. The problem is, kids will copy the behavior they see in pro athletes, whether it's Pascual Perez throwing at a hitter, or hockey players trying to behead each other with their sticks, or, most serious of all, players getting in trouble with drugs. A kid concludes it's no big deal, the players don't get arrested, they just go to a rehab center. "Why can't I do drugs, too?"

Athletes may not be heroes to the extent they once were, but they're still role models, and they have a huge responsibility as such. That's why the fighting and the drugs have got to be eliminated. Especially the drugs.

What galls me is when an athlete claims it's a violation of his civil rights to require him to take a urinalysis. Hell, we all take that test every time we go to the doctor. Players get tested in their preseason physicals. It is emphatically *not* an infringement. A ballplayer has a signed contract binding the team to pay him and committing him to give his mental and physical best. If the employer has medical evidence that shows the player is impaired by an illegal substance, the player should be held to be in violation of his contract. It's an infringement of the club agreement to have a player spaced out on drugs and muttering, "Hey, man, where's the ball, I can't see shit."

Let me repeat. I want this clearly understood: It is not dehumanizing to pee into a bottle. If a jock can't figure that out, let's put it in language he can't misunderstand: M-O-N-E-Y. If you're messed up, you don't get paid. Athletes say being on stuff doesn't affect performance. That is irrational and just plain wrong. Most of the guys who get on cocaine can't get off, even with the best medical help available. How can they argue it doesn't affect their performance? It affects their whole life! Coke owns you. Richard Pryor has a wonderfully dramatic routine about cocaine. He's in his room, alone with his drug. "Richard, what are you going to do today? You're gonna smoke me, aren't you?" As another comic said, "Cocaine is God's way of telling you that you have too much money." I don't know much about marijuana or other drugs, but I know damn well you can't get off cocaine by yourself. The dehumanizing thing is not mandatory drug testing; it's when the fan sees a guy trip on a perfect field and figures it's because the player was high. Once the trust of the paying customer is lost, it's over, and baseball commissioner Peter Ueberroth knows that.

How come athletes are so dumb as to risk their multimillion-dollar futures by using coke? I think there's an easy answer to that question. Because it feels good. I heard Mort Sahl doing a takeoff that contained some fundamental truths on this subject. The gist of it was, drugs make you feel good, which is OK. But if you do nothing but feel good all day, you become a junkie and a worthless human being. You won't do anything *but* feel good all the time. You owe more to society than that. If you break the law, you get nailed. If you can't perform your job, you get fired. There is nothing inconsistent here.

Certainly there's a lot of organized pressure to make sure we never feel good. Some of it is church-related. If sex makes you feel good, it's bad, according to a centuries-old school of thought. We can reject some of that by saying if a practice hurts no one, it's legitimate in the privacy of one's home. But when an athlete starts to infringe on his contract and is incapable of performing his job, it's time for the authorities to say, "Time out. End of game. You're hurting your family and your team, and you're setting a terrible example for the youth of this country." If all this isn't enough reason to crack down on drug use once and for all, I don't know what the hell is.

It's true that many players come from deprived

backgrounds and never had $20 in their pocket until they reached the big leagues. Suddenly they have a lot of money, and they're followed by scum selling drugs in hotel lobbies. I've heard drugs were even for sale at the arena in Oakland. *Sports Illustrated* once had an article by a former Charger, Don Reese, who called them a dirty team and said drug use was rampant. At the time, Gene Klein denied the story, but after the club was sold, he recanted and said he believed it.

Something is badly out of synch here. I can understand why management must protect its players up to a point, but there were reports that several Charger players asked teammates to take their urinalysis for them at preseason physicals in 1984. I happen to believe drug use is even more out of hand than has been reported. I mean, if we know of 20 documented cases, how many more have been covered up? It must be at epidemic proportions if we're catching as many as we are. There could be ten violators for every one detected.

It's absurd for an athlete who makes a living with his body to poison it by putting illegal chemicals in it. If he can't or won't quit on his own, the club has every right to take action against him. I am almost invariably pro-athlete, but not on this issue. For years we have seen clubs pay for the best doctors and rehabilitation centers and psychoanalysis, and pay full salary through it all. Enough is enough. The clubs have gone the extra mile. Now it's time to say to the players: "You're finished."

I don't want to sound heartless, but we're now seeing athletes being welcomed back into the fold after three or four relapses, and that has got to stop. I'm talking about basketball players like John Lucas and John Drew. Houston Coach Bill Fitch said he didn't believe in giving a second chance to any drug violator, so why did he grant a third chance to Lucas — could it have been to help his team's playoff chances?

I happen to believe in a second chance for everyone. We all make mistakes. We live in a forgiving country, and we should be thankful for that. But this business of a third and fourth chance for an athlete is ludicrous. How long can it go on? The clubs have got to start saying, "You blew it, pal. You're off this team."

Having been in the sports biz for 15 years, I am cynical enough to doubt that the crackdown is going to arrive soon. There's been so much tolerance for so long. I used to wonder why ballplayers would walk around drinking coffee out of a styrofoam cup during batting practice. Then somebody told me it was because they had taken their greenies (amphetamines) and were using the caffeine to make it kick in sooner. And that's the truth. For years greenies were laid out on the trainer's table for any player to take. I think amphetamine use dropped off to an extent because players realized it did not enhance performance as much as they expected. Now there's an explosion of steroid use because players think it will help them get bigger and stronger. Of course it also destroys the kidneys and liver, causes hypertension, and has other unpleasant side effects.

With steroids, as opposed to cocaine, I can understand the financial imperative. There was a survey before the Olympics in which athletes were asked if they would continue to take steroids even if it were shown the drugs caused sterility, blindness, and death. A majority said they would take steroids if it would guarantee a gold medal. That says it all about athletes being willing to do anything — cheat, take drugs, whatever — in order to win. It's truly a monstrous thing when the choice is between a gold medal and a healthy life.

Whether they're clean livers or not, why do athletes feel so much pressure to succeed? If we narrow the discussion to the so-called "sphere of amateur athletics," I think a lot of the pressure is just wanting to be the best. Economics, however, is part of the equation, with athletes observing the riches that have been bestowed upon the successful.

I hope amateur athletes who aspire to wealth will realize that the Bruce Jenners and Mary Lou Rettons of the world aren't succeeding financially just because they're terrific athletes. Both Jenner and Retton, for example, are white, photogenic, and terrific with the media. The advertisers didn't seem to want much to do with other gold medal winners in recent Olympics. Carl Lewis, for example, didn't make peanuts after his four gold medals at the 1984 games.

Carl is a classic case of the athlete blaming the press for his problems. He claimed he didn't get endorsements because the media painted him as arrogant. He had tried to market himself in the Jenner mold. Rather, his marketing team had tried to pull off that feat. But I think Americans got tired of being told how Carl would only settle for the class accounts, like Coca Cola, Wheaties, and E. F. Hutton, if he did well at the Olympics. Carl should have pinned the blame on his agent, his attorney, and his marketing man, who packaged him like a bar of soap or a box of tampons.

Carl wouldn't do interviews at the Olympics, even though the world press corps was there in force. He said he would talk every other Wednesday, or something like that. Gee, Carl, if my knees weren't so sore, I'd kneel down and bow. Carl wouldn't practice with his relay team, and he didn't want to live in the Olympic Village with his teammates. He was loudly booed by fans who paid $100 for tickets to watch him bow out of the long jump after just one leap. After winning his fourth medal, he spotted a giant American flag in the stands and carried it around the track on a victory lap. Even that gesture came off flat, looking as if it had been staged, which no doubt it was.

A couple of writers I respect, Jim Murray and Wayne Lockwood, defended Lewis, asking why we as Americans are never satisfied and why we put so much pressure on our athletes. The thing is, Americans will let you endorse products and take the money, but they can't stand arrogance. They'd rather root for the underdog. They turned their backs on Carl Lewis, and consequently Madison Avenue wouldn't touch him. For this, he has only himself and his advisers to blame.

Mary Decker must likewise be included in the same condemnation. With only the slightest bit of introspection, she should be able to ask herself why even her teammates criticized her public whining. Instead, she preferred to blame Zola Budd for the accident in the Olympic race. She failed to understand that Americans like to see a little humility and good sportsmanship in their heroes. They'll give you the $1 million paycheck, but they don't like arrogant winners or resentful losers. Mary wouldn't apologize to Zola, and then she wondered why the endorsement money dried up. We all have flaws. But Mary won't admit to hers.

The Edwin Moses story is different. For whatever foibles and frailties he has shown — and he was acquitted on charges of soliciting a prostitute — he probably will earn more endorsements and respect. He was caught in an embarrassing situation, but he didn't alibi, and he managed to come off as an underdog, which he had never been on a track. Americans can be demanding, but they can also be very forgiving. I think Moses will be the recipient of love and respect that Mary Decker and Carl Lewis can only dream about. Moses may have to put up with some references in the Johnny Carson monologues for years to come, but Americans are going to bend over backward to forgive him. I don't know why more athletes don't understand that it makes such a crucial difference to admit your flaws and relate to the public.

While we're discussing the Olympics, I'd like to say they should be done away with entirely, and tomorrow would be fine timing. Peter Ueberroth was named *Time* magazine's man of the year for his role in staging the 1984 Olympics, but even in this tale, there was hypocrisy by the shovelful. Ueberroth, a so-called volunteer, wound up making about $1 million from the Olympics in salary and bonus, while the decision was made to trim the budget for training future athletes.

I don't know a clearer way to put this: the Olympics are crap. Please take the Olympics and flush them. They are too big and too political. I don't know how Seoul could have been awarded the 1988 games. How stupid to stage the games in a troubled nation that can't feed its people and is now compelled to spend many millions to build athletic facilities. It's going to be a boondoggle, and I suspect the Russians would agree. It has been proposed to take politics out of the Olympics, but how is that to be accomplished? When an athlete wins a medal, they raise a flag and play an anthem, right? What this says is childish: "I won, my flag flies. You lost, yours doesn't. Nah nah nah." Worse, we see communist nations training kids from infancy and using the Olympics as a propaganda tool. "Sure we send millions to gulags, but we win gold medals, so our system works." With that mind set, we play right into their hands by investing the Olympics with so much importance. We're stupid to even be in the Olympic movement.

Americans delude themselves by recalling the splendor that was Los Angeles in August 1984. We won multiple gold medals, but would we have done so if the Russians had been present? Of course not. Look, I know the Russians are a menace to world peace, but let's face it, they do have some tremendous athletes. If not for the Russian boycott, there's no way we could have won half as many gold medals in L. A. The competition made the wins inconclusive. So why don't we stop this nonsense? The Olympics are a dumb exercise in futility. They should be put out of their misery. Immediately.

CHAPTER 19

Tremors on Park Avenue

One of the more dramatic turnabouts in recent San Diego sports history concerns the ownership of the Chargers and its attitude toward public enemy number one. The previous owner, Gene Klein, had the utmost contempt for Al Davis and the Los Angeles Raiders, whereas his successor, Alex Spanos, is a friend and admirer of Davis. To see this relationship played out in the next couple of years should be most entertaining for Charger fans. I doubt that we'll ever see the Raiders become favorites in Mission Valley, but the intensity of the rivalry may lessen a bit. The players, incidentally, never hated each other the way Klein and Davis did.

Say what you will about Al Davis, but the man just will not allow himself to be beaten, on the field, in court, or in any other aspect of life. That commitment to winning is something other owners should study and emulate. You simply should not be in the sports business these days if you don't have it, because you're facing an array of unions, arbitrators, and free agents who can sap your desire for excellence if all you look at is the bottom line. You have to be conscious of running your operation as a business, but you cannot be in sports simply to make money. If E. F. Hutton ever advised a businessman to buy an NFL franchise, the business community at large would stop listening. You have to put pride and love for the game ahead of the dollar. When the Raiders last went to the Super Bowl, Davis chartered a couple of jets to take the team and his entourage, and wound up spending more than $1 million. It wasn't a bottom-line decision. He wanted to buy the biggest rings, throw the best party, and impress his friends. That's why you're in sports, anyway, for the ego boost and to bask in the reflected glory of the athletes.

Gene Klein didn't treat it that way, and I don't how Spanos will pan out. Al Davis, though, is committed to excellence. And now, having built him up to a certain extent, I'd like to say that I do not have much respect for his methods. He'll do anything to win, even if it involves bending the rules. He once likened himself to Hitler in his thinking on overwhelming the opposition. In a book by the late Jack Murphy entitled *Damn You, Al Davis* the Raiders owner had Harland Svare,the Charger coach at the time, believing he had planted a microphone in the locker room so he could eavesdrop on the game plan. I don't know if Davis actually was guilty as charged, but I'm sure the idea would appeal greatly to him as a tactical weapon.

From the black uniforms and the skull and cross bones on the helmets, the Raiders really buffalo the opposition with their image. I'm sure Davis revels in intimidating young players on opposing teams.

I tend to side with him in his conflict with the NFL. I really think if you have a team, you have a right to put it wherever you want. How can the league claim it's a giant partnership when each team is in business to beat the others? I think they're individual businesses trying to win and make some money. They're an association certainly, but no different from an association of plumbers who gather at a convention once a year to discuss general concepts of doing business. The NFL owners are not in business to make money for the league as a whole. They do need money to lobby in Washington and buy off Congressmen, but in essence they're in business as individuals. It fractures most of these guys that Al Davis is a little smarter and always finds ways to beat them. I admire his total commitment, even if I don't admire his methods.

Davis had every right to say the NFL could not prevent him from leaving Oakland and moving to Los Angeles. He's something of a visionary, and the enormous cable TV market appealed to him. How in the hell can anyone in a free enterprise system deny a fellow businessman the chance to make a buck? The hypocrisy — there's that word again — is mind boggling. In the last couple of years there has been consideration in Congress of legislation that would regulate the movement of sports franchises. If the truth be known, the Congressmen don't give a damn about the issue except as it relates to their own prospects of reelection. Each one just wants to make sure there's a team in his or her city, and the hell with anyone else's city. For example, in 1984, we saw legislation sponsored by Missouri representatives, which happened to come at a time when it was feared the Cardinals might move from St. Louis.

Later we saw legislation introduced by Senator Arlen Specter of Pennsylvania when there was fear the Eagles might move from Philadelphia. Specter, who is virtually owned by the National Football League, was the same guy who once introduced a bill to prohibit undergraduate Herschel Walker from turning pro before his college class graduated. His interest, we may be sure, was not in seeing that college students graduate.

He simply wanted to make sure the stars couldn't leave early for the USFL, and thus deny the NFL a chance to draft them. If that concept is not unconstitutional, I will eat a copy of this book. "You can't make a living in your chosen field until we say you can." That's the NFL posture, and if that's not in restraint of trade, I don't have the slightest grasp of the concept. It's precisely the same thing as telling a bright young banker about to graduate from college that he will be subject to a draft of national banks, and if the bank in Keokuk, Iowa, selects him, he will report for work on an assigned date and work for whatever wage they stipulate. That's exactly what the NFL does, and it has Congressmen perpetuating the system. No player is going to give up two or three prime years of his career and spend $1 million in legal fees to challenge the system. I'm on the side of the players, who have absolutely no leverage, and it makes me insanely mad when I realize our Congressmen are devoting their tax-subsidized time to aiding and abetting the NFL, when they ought to be more concerned about human starvation and nuclear proliferation.

I look for Phoenix to get a pro football franchise in the near future because an Arizona representative introduced another of these proposed regulations to limit movement of sports franchises, as the NFL wanted. The NFL gets its antitrust exemption, and the guys who help get a franchise. That's the reality.

While I'm willing to grant a sports franchise the freedom to do business in the city of its choice, that same franchise cannot expect concessions or demand the love and trust of the fans. The franchise must not expect a city to pour millions into building a stadium if it can't count on having a tenant. You can't have it both ways in a truly open market. How can you let the import quota on foreign cars expire and limit the movement of sports franchises? These Congressmen, who fly home at tax-payer expense to watch the boys play on Sunday, have got to realize what we have is an open market.

The owners have got to understand that there is no hope of loyalty on the part of the fans if the team has the license to relocate on a whim. Don't tell me about the loyalty that existed in the old days. This isn't family, this is business. The only loyalty is to the dollar bill. Loyalty has nothing to do with the equation anymore.

One of the more compelling case studies in the an-nals of free enterprise concerns the former owner of the Philadelphia Eagles, Mr. Leonard Tose. I know him fairly well, because I used to announce Eagles games, and I also double-dated with him and his girl friend. On one memorable weekend when the Eagles were sched-uled to play an exhibition game in San Diego, he took a helicopter from his office to the airport, where a chartered jet was waiting to fly the team to the West Coast. In San Diego he rented a suite in the Hyatt Islan-dia and hosted a buffet featuring shrimp as big as buffalo. His life style never changed, even when his gambling debts ran into the multimillions. And he was allowed to retain ownership of the Eagles, even though NFL Commissioner Pete Rozelle must have known what was going on. Rozelle told him to stop, and Tose prom-ised he would, but he didn't. He wound up selling the team to a group from Miami after failing to work out a deal with some Philadelphians, who offered $56 million for the Eagles. Tose then had the nerve to ask to remain in charge of the team at a salary of $600,000 a year plus expenses of $150,000.

Now let's consider the main issue raised by the Tose case. It was well known that he had gambling debts of enormous proportions. And he was by no means the only member of the sports establishment to indulge in this pastime. George Steinbrenner owns a horse track in Florida, where there's lots of betting. The Galbraith family, which owns the Pittsburgh Pirates, raises racehorses. All pro sports leagues want to distance themselves from ties with gambling, at least at the level of the players, but they have a different standard as far as owners are concerned.

My theory on gambling is that it's like drug use. If so many people are talking about it, and we see a few getting caught, how many are really doing it? I don't know how the lid has been kept in place for so long. They theorize that $1 billion is wagered on the Super Bowl alone in friendly bets — not counting Las Vegas and the bookies. Hundreds of millions are bet every weekend of the season. You can't tell me the players are totally clean. I mean, Paul Hornung was caught 20 years ago, and Art Schlichter came forward a few years ago when he couldn't pay off his gambling debts and consequently his life was endangered.

When the scandal breaks in pro sports, it's going to be very messy and very damaging. It will make the drug thing seem minor. Most fans don't really give a damn about drugs, anyway. It only bothers them if they think the outcome of a game — a bet — was influenced by some guy on dope. The fans shrug off drug use unless it hits them in the wallet. If a guy wants to blow out his nasal cavities with cocaine, the average fan just shrugs it off as another dumb jock wasting his natural talent.

But when and if the gambling dollars of millions of fans are tainted by rigged games, it will result in a scandal that could blow Pete Rozelle right off Park Avenue. Believe me, he's aware of it, and will do all in his power to suppress gambling, or any hint of gambling, by players.

I'm vaguely amused, and a little irritated, by newspapers that do commentaries on the terrible gambling problem, and then two pages later print the latest line from Las Vegas. I don't mean to pick on the print media. Television stations are also guilty. In fact, I've picked games myself. I used to do something called the Leitner Line. The news director suggested it, and I went along with it. I hope people in office pools weren't comparing their bets to my line, but they probably were. When I worked in Hartford, I even did a little gambling of my own. A friend knew a bookie, and I would bet $50 a weekend on three games. I have to admit I'd then sit at home screaming at the TV when there was a game I had a wager on. But I quickly found it wasn't enjoyable or profitable, and I haven't done any betting since 1975. I felt the hook enough to see how it can become a compulsive thing.

Gambling, as far as I know, is against the law in most states, yet newspapers and TV are promoting it. Even the networks do it with guys like Jimmy the Greek picking games. You know damn well if the NFL didn't want a buffoon like the Greek on TV, he'd be off the air yesterday. Yet, when the scandal hits, the NFL will say it couldn't believe this stuff was actually going on.

People gushed over how courageous Art Schlichter was for admitting his gambling, but, hey, he owed the mob hundreds of thousands, and they were going to waste him. He came forward out of desperation and was granted immunity from prosecution. How is that to be considered courageous? I don't mean to pick on him. I happen to believe he has plenty of company in all sports. There's no way he's alone in wagering on games.

I'll never forget a New York Knicks game several years ago. In the last minute Earl Monroe shot the ball into the wrong basket, and it affected the line. There were a lot of raised eyebrows.

We've witnessed major scandals in college basketball in the 1950s and again in 1985. Kids at Tulane were impressed by a couple of hundred bucks a game. If they would shave points for that, imagine what would happen if they were approached by some short, swarthy moron with a long cigar, offering drugs, women, and cash to fix a game. There must be a Tulane a year, at least. The NCAA actually got around to talking some tough sanctions, such as banning a university from competition for a year or two. But you read the fine print and you'll see a school would have to be caught several times to incur the tough penalty. Nobody ever gets caught twice in the NCAA, so the new rules are, in effect, meaningless. The rules, of course, are made by coaches and ex-coaches, good old boys who look after one another. They're not going to institute any really punitive actions against themselves. The NFL is no different. Through its high-powered public relations machinery, the NFL would do its best to cover up any hint of gambling. It's going to be very tough to find evidence of gambling in pro sports, but I believe it's inevitable.

CHAPTER 20

Cleaning Up

I want to tell you about a broadcaster's nightmare. I saw a movie in which the male lead picked up a woman who was obviously intent on seducing him. The next morning the man heard a tapping at his door. "Open up! Police!" The woman had cried rape. My mouth fell open. What's to prevent a similar injustice from wrecking *my* life? I could meet someone at a cocktail party and inadvertently come across as arrogant, rude, or a hotshot. It doesn't require an overactive imagination to visualize the possibilities. Thus, I live in dread fear of being falsely accused — of anything. It happens, you know. Our judicial system is the best there is, but it's not infallible. I don't want to be trapped by someone else's mistake. I can hear the words now: "Well, I thought it was a guy with glasses and kinky hair. Sorry." So my career is screwed. Sorry.

My fear is distantly related to what Edwin Moses had to face after being arrested and charged with soliciting prostitution. Moses knew there were going to be jokes and more jokes about his misfortune. I'm not usually so fortunate. There would be jokes, sure, but that would be just the beginning of it. If I get charged with something illegal, my career is done, even if I'm acquitted. An athlete can get cleaned up and resume his career. Not me. In this country we're presumed to be innocent until proven guilty, but I'm quite sure I would be judged guilty as soon as the charges were filed. So I have to be squeaky clean, above suspicion.

I stay as far away from drugs as I can. I can honestly say I have never seen cocaine. I was in a bar one New Year's Eve and somebody pulled out a little vial that contained a powdery substance that I knew wasn't Fab or Ajax. This guy was no Robert Redford, but he had a couple of ultra-nice women hanging on him, and every half hour or so one of them would disappear into the restroom with that little vial. After observing this behavior, I realized I should get the hell out of there.

I have never held any coke or seen it on a coffee table and I certainly have never put it in my nose. I've seen it on TV after someone gets busted and the cops march the suspects, wearing handcuffs and with their faces covered, out to the squad car for the trip downtown. I remember watching coverage of a big drug bust in early 1985, when the authorities announced they were going to obtain a list of users and suppliers from the guys they arrested. My initial reaction was, "Right on. Get rid of this crap."

Then I had a second thought. What if there was a dealer who had seen me on TV and decided he didn't like me. To save his ass, he could tell the district attorney I was one of his customers. He could start naming every big name in town, and if he had happened to watch my sports segment, my name might be fresh in his memory. If I ever made one of those lists, I'd be done.

There's a standard clause in a broadcaster's contract covering moral turpitude. But, to cover myself, I had the clause modified to say I had to be indicted or convicted in order for the contract to be voided.

Athletes and entertainers can emerge from a rehab center or walk out of jail and go back to work, but an announcer on local TV enjoys no such freedom.

I pay my taxes, even if it costs some extra thousands I might get around if I searched for loopholes. The thought of doing something that might be considered illegal makes me pay and pay some more. Fear is my motivation. I've been hard on athletes for so long. A regular feature of my show is the police blotter, where I recite the details of athletes in trouble with the law. I rant and rave from the heart, but it doesn't leave much margin for error in my personal life. I sometimes wake up in a cold sweat after a bad dream in which this voice says, "See, there's big mouth! Look what he did! Serves him right that he got caught!"

When I was in Hartford, there were two brothers from Sweden playing hockey for the Whalers, and they were featured on a commercial plugging a local car dealer. "Yah, yah, we buy Volvo, we reeely like Volvo." Everybody in town recognized the brothers. Then one day they were arrested for driving without a license, and I couldn't wait to get to the station and try out a few cute lines. "Driver's license? Ve have no driver's license. Vat is driver's license?" I was hard on them, but I was being flip. I certainly wouldn't want to have the situation reversed and have need for legal representation.

I've been known to come down rather hard on agents and attorneys, but I really don't detest them. The classic definition of waste comes from Bum Phillips, the New Orleans Saints coach. "Waste," Bum said, "is when a busload of attorneys goes over a cliff and there are two empty seats." Sorry, Bum, I have to disagree. I think three empty seats would be a bit closer. I went through a divorce proceeding that never even went to trial, and the attorney's bill came to $7,000. There were no depositions, no meetings with a judge, probably not five hours of work. I once used the Bum Phillips line at a speech that was reported by the *Daily Transcript*. The next issue contained several letters from indignant attorneys attacking me, not Bum. Where's the justice in that, I ask. There are good cops and bad cops, good attorneys and those who'll bill you $200 if you pick up the phone and sneeze.

In sports, the situation with agents and attorneys has reached the point of scandal. There are more agents than coaches at college all-star games. These guys offer drugs, women, loans, cars, anything to line up business. I'm expecting to open *The Sporting News* any day now and read an ad that says, "Hi, I would like to represent you. Give me a call at 1-800-BULLSHIT." The only way to get business, other than through a reputation for excellence, is get out and hobnob, and we have already noted that most 20-year-old athletes are not comparable to William F. Buckley in cerebral development. Some kids have signed with two or three agents and taken loans from all of them.

It's dishonest for a college athlete to sign with an agent before his eligibility is complete, but I have to laugh when a kid from East Toiletseat dumps a Manhattan agent after being wooed for a year with an apartment, car, money, and broads. I do like to see the shysters get out-shystered. Justice may be crude and uneven, but it's still justice. What's happening is scandalous, but I don't have a solution except to do a better job of educating America's college athlete. That isn't likely, so who's going to help these kids? Unless a guy selects a reputable agent like Howard Slusher, Leigh Steinberg, or Bob Woolf, he can end up in trouble. If nothing else, the leagues should establish a referral agency.

The clubs, of course, would prefer that no athlete had an agent. This goes back to the time when Jim Ringo, the center for the Green Bay Packers, hired an agent, who went in to bargain with Vince Lombardi. Lombardi asked to be excused to make a phone call, then 30 minutes later announced to the agent that Ringo had been traded to the Philadelphia Eagles. That was sort of like Gene Klein trading John Jefferson to Green Bay. Red Auerbach could be just as tough on members of the Boston Celtics. Jim Barnes once asked for a yellow Cadillac, and Red threw him out of his office.

Buzzie Bavasi was one of the all-time bargainers in baseball. With the Dodgers, Padres, and Angels, he abused his share of players, and then some. His most infamous trick was to draw up a phony contract with, say, Duke Snider, and have it on his desk when a lesser player came in to negotiate. Buzzie would get up and leave for 10 minutes, and the player couldn't help but see the contract, which might be for half of what Snider was really being paid. "Holy, shit! If the Duke is only getting 40 grand, I better take what Buzzie is offering me before he decides to cut it."

Baseball, as an industry, treated its stars and backups with disdain for decades. The year Joe DiMaggio hit in 56 straight games, he was offered a contract for $1,000 less than he made the previous season. The Yankees tried to cut Mickey Mantle a year after he hit .365. With that kind of history, baseball deserves what it's getting from agents. The sad thing is that today's crop doesn't seem to realize what earlier players endured. Curt Flood of the St. Louis Cardinals paved the way by challenging the reserve clause and winning the case before the Supreme Court. You might think the players association would be happy to buy him a house, but I doubt if that's the case.

Want to know how insensitive ballplayers can be? The Detroit Tigers didn't even vote a full share of World Series money to their traveling secretary, the man who nursemaids them, makes all their travel arrangements and checks their luggage, takes care of all their needs. In the old days the players didn't get much. Today they don't appreciate what they have. The owners claim they're awash in red ink, but they brought it on themselves with decades of handling the athletes by the short hairs.

What amazes me is how the fan always seems to side with the owners. It's easy to be critical of a ballplayer wanting a Rolls Royce as a signing bonus, but in the final analysis, the player is going to get his share, or the owner is going to keep all of it. The fans see themselves, and rightly so, as laborers, fighting for raises all their lives, and you'd think they'd identify with the ballplayers. But it's not that way. The fan would rather see Tony Gwynn make less and Joan Kroc make more. I suppose the poor and the middle class in America have just accepted that it's supposed to be this way: the rich are supposed to have their money, and nobody else is. George Steinbrenner has his shipbuilding business, the owner of the Detroit Tigers has his pizza chain. The fans accept that. It drives the fans nuts to see a player, who is perceived as an equal of the fan, becoming wealthy. "I was a high school jock, I could have done what that guy did if I'd had a break. That son of a bitch is making $1 million a year now. Well, screw him." The salaries may be ludicrous, but that's America, that's capitalism. The players didn't start it. I'll always side with the players.

And I will solemnly maintain, at least until the day they unplug my mike, that the great issues of our time have nothing to do with what happens on artificial turf. If you want something serious and laden with meaning, read a Tolstoy novel. Yesterday's scores, like yesterday's news, are easily forgotten. Games are a diversion — useful in that respect, but limited in a way. If any of you serious sports fans are still with us, ease up, would you? Have a little fun. A game is only a game.

Ted Leitner, who needs no introduction, is sports director of KFMB TV. He is also the voice of the San Diego Chargers' radio network, and is frequently heard on broadcasts of San Diego Padres' games. Among his hobbies are sandwiches, sunshine, and jogging.

Chris Cobbs is a sports writer for the San Diego edition of the *Los Angeles Times*. His assignments include coverage of the Chargers and a variety of feature topics.

More Sports Titles
for Your Enjoyment!

SPIKE! by Doug Beal
The Story of the Victorious U.S. Volleyball Team, by their coach

Spike! takes us behind the scenes and on the court with the team, their coach, and the high-pressure atmosphere surrounding the emergence of the world-class team.

Doug Beal tells the story of the team's quest for the gold medal. He provides the reader with insights and perceptions about his players, offers analyses of other teams, and relates, in technical terms, how the Americans finally captured the gold medal in their thrilling match against Brazil. And he candidly chronicles the controversial nature of his demanding year-round program, its financial troubles, and its evolution into a successful model for similar programs. **$9.95 6 x 9 paperback, 176 pp., including 32 pages of action photos.**

The Famous Chicken Baseball Quiz Book by Ted Giannoulas (The Famous Chicken) & Andy Strasberg, (Director of Marketing, San Diego Padres)

From the moment he stepped into his famous chicken costume a decade ago, Ted Giannoulas has brought laughter, spirit, and delight to sports fans throughout the world. Acclaimed as one of the most talented mimes in entertainment today, the Chicken performs before audiences totalling 5,000,000 annually.

As part of his tenth anniversary celebration, Ted Giannoulas, in collaboration with Andy Strasberg, has written *The Famous Chicken Baseball Quiz Book*, a question and answer trivia book for the entire family.

This entertaining and informative collection of questions includes true-false, multiple choice, quotation matching, and photo game sections. **$2.95 4½ x 7 paperback, 140 pp.**

AVAILABLE AT YOUR LOCAL BOOKSTORE, OR FROM
AVANT BOOKS
3719 SIXTH AVENUE
SAN DIEGO, CA 92109-4316
Add $1.00 for first book and $.50 for each additional for shipping/handling (add 6% sales tax — California only).